Hunted in the Heartland

A MEMOIR OF MURDER

Bonney Hogue Patterson

bluebird
PUBLISHING

Bluebird Publishing, a division of Virginia Publishing Company
PO Box 4538
St. Louis, MO 63108
www.STL-Books.com
www.Bluebirdbookpub.com

Contents

Acknowledgements

I particularly want to thank Detective Christina Morrow of the Marion, Illinois, Police Department for her patience and the time she devoted to answering my queries. After all these years, finally, *I* got to be the one asking questions and receiving answers from the police, instead of the other way around. That those answers were not always what I wanted to hear is of course no one's fault. She is a credit to her department.

I also want to thank Lieutenant Paul Echols of the Carbondale Police Department. A more organized, dedicated individual I have never met, and without him I doubt any of the heinous crimes committed by Timothy Krajcir would have ever been solved. Thanks for speaking with me, but I hope we don't meet again because of similar circumstances. I know if *I* decide to commit any serious crimes, it will not be in your town!

Detective Jimmy Smith of the Cape Girardeau, Missouri Police Department was very helpful in opening my eyes to Krajcir's crimes committed here in my adoptive state. Luckily, I was able to follow the many twists and turns of Krajcir's criminal life beyond Marion, Illinois, because he was the trailblazer. His experience and intuition told him that Krajcir was involved with some of the cold cases he was dealing with, and he was right.

We are very lucky to have such smart, efficient and effective law protection officers working on our behalf. You are heroes, in my humble estimation.

I also want to thank a very special person, independent editor Rob Kaplan. The first person I worked with, he was invaluable not only for his organizational ability, but wonderfully insightful. Sometimes the questions,--why did I do that, or who said what to whom, and so forth--nearly drove me crazy, but it is a better book because he took such an interest. I couldn't gloss over anything without asking, "Why?" of myself, because he held me accountable. I hope this finished product is to his liking. Now you can stop discussing murder and mayhem over dinner with the family, Rob.

Also, I want to give a special acknowledgement to my ex-neighbor, Connie Clark, for sharing a tumultuous time. She gave the police every ounce of cooperation they could possibly have hoped for and then some. Also, thanks for your support and encouragement for both the story to be told and to me while writing it. And, to the neighbors from that time whom I spoke to, especially Sherry Austin, thanks for sharing your memories and information with me.

Thanks to my daughter, Sarah, for reading nonstop, even though you said it kept you up all night. And thanks to now grown-up baby Jeffy, who no longer needs his mommy to defend him, but has gone on to the war in Afghanistan to defend us all.

And, needless to say, many thanks go to my husband of years and years, Roger. Who else would ever put up with me? How many men could take in stride that his wife all of a sudden knew who had killed their neighbor almost thirty years ago, almost immediately after suffering a terrible fall and concussion? Par for the course, of course.

Also, a *big* thanks to Catherine Rankovic for helping me through the final edit. You may well have saved my sanity, Catherine.

Introduction

A book about a man who was a highly efficient, evil predator upon women, a serial killer, no less, this is essentially a story told from a women's, and a community's, points of view. It has elements of investigative work and forensic evidence, inside police stories, and on occasion delves into the mind and background of this criminal. It became necessary to dig fairly deeply into police records and track down individuals who played a part in a baffling and brutal murder investigation. It evolved that this one murder, in my neighborhood, and the ensuing investigation, presented a crucial, and unique, pivotal point at which a serial killer could have been stopped. Five additional victims would have kept their lives, and much misery experienced by the survivors of his violent, deviant assaults, would have been spared their trauma. That one life caused so much grief for so many for so long is incredible.

It begins as one woman's story and that of her family and neighbors unwittingly pulled into a shocking murder investigation. It reignited years later after confessions from this sexual predator and killer of nine women, as a simple desire to get answers from police who, years ago, had asked us plenty of questions, but gave little to no information in return. This murder that happened in the middle of the day, literally under our noses as our children played outside and we gardened in our yards, was unfortunately destined to become a cold case for many years.

Incredibly, the answers I did receive after Timothy Krajcir's confessions were sometimes unsettling and jarring. It was not a neat process, asking questions and finally receiving satisfying answers. With a prison record, but still virtually unchecked, Krajcir freely spread mayhem, degradation, and murder for years.

I began to feel I was following a thread through a jungle—there were more bewildering twists and turns than I could ever have imagined, certainly more than I could ever have made up. Beginning with a confession to one murder, other victims quickly emerged, all bound together by their fateful encounters with Krajcir. I picked up the end of the thread and followed it back to where it belonged, rewinding as I went.

Now I know to which spool my thread belongs, and where that spool is. Finally, after nearly three decades, a face, a name and a sense of who this criminal is who so brutally shattered our peace and tranquility, "hunting" our very neighborhood for his next victim, and, finding what he came for, taking my neighbor's life away with him. Now I know where that spool will remain. Forever.

Gobsmacked

Definition: flabbergasted, astounded.
Etymology: from gob 'mouth' + smacked 'clapping hand over in surprise',
Webster's New Millennium "Dictionary of English, Preview Edition (v 0.97)

December 10, 2007

I awoke early to a gray, icy morning. Freezing rain had visited during the night in St. Charles County, Missouri. I turned on my television set to check for school closings as I was due at the local high school before 7 a.m. for my substitute teaching job. Keeping one eye on the scrawl at the bottom of the newscast for the school closings, I readied myself to go. With one last glance at the television screen for my school, I left. Class wasn't cancelled today, it seemed.

Occasional patches of black ice lurked on the roadway ready to send the unwary into nearby ditches or other obstacles.

I approached the school parking lot and did not see any buses. Perhaps we had gone to a late-start-day schedule. Several teachers had arrived, and a group of them and a few administrators were gathered outside the front door. I parked in my usual spot and approached the group.

The Principal announced that there would be no school today. The school district had made the decision too late to get the information out to the media. He said we could come in for awhile, or we could go home. A couple of people turned to go, including another substitute teacher. She slipped a little on the ice.

1

"Be careful!" I urged. She made it back to her car without further incident.

After a few pleasantries, I turned to leave. I never felt the fall, never even had a sensation of falling, only that of my right foot slipping on a patch of ice. Then there was the sudden impact of the back of my head hitting the pavement. I was laid out on the icy cold, wet sidewalk, unable to get up without assistance. I vaguely heard someone saying, "Call 9-1-1."

Feeling no pain as yet, I was nevertheless shocked and astounded by the force of the blow to the back of my head. *Gobsmacked*, with a capital "G".

Never before had I had the experience of being in an ER trauma center during a snow and ice storm. While under observation in a small room beside the nurse's station for my head injury, I watched all day as the wounded were brought in, x-rayed, scanned, splinted, bandaged, stitched, medicated and sent on their way.

I had a concussion, neck, rib, collarbone and lower back injuries, but x-rays showed no broken bones, luckily.

Around mid-day I asked, a couple of times, for the nurse to turn off the overhead light. It was so bright I felt it was making my headache worse. And a nap seemed like such a good idea, because I was tired and sleepy. Even with the bustle going on outside, I thought I could easily drift off, if not for that annoyingly bright overhead light. Of course, the nurses had no intention of giving me a dark or quiet room, I realized later. Going to sleep was the *last* thing they wanted for a patient with a head injury.

But, even as I was pleading for a darkened room, I had no idea, then, that another, equally jarring event was taking place at that very same time in southern Illinois, in an equally busy, bright setting. A man was facing a judge and making his own plea—of murder.

My husband, Roger, came to the hospital to see me home late that afternoon. Once safely back at our house, I finally took some pain medication. Everything hurt, and I had a whopper of a headache. While nibbling at a light dinner, I was half-listening to the evening news as I glanced through that morning's newspaper.

One of the big news stories of the day appeared to be a

break in a cold-case murder in Carbondale, Illinois. A man had pled guilty today of murdering a young college co-ed. DNA had linked this with a suspect, already in prison.

I turned to Roger and said, "I bet this has something to do with the Virginia Witte murder."

Surprised at this out-of-the-blue statement, he responded, "Haven't you had a busy enough day without trying to solve an almost 30-year-old murder?"

That night I slept fitfully. My shoulders, head, back, collarbone and neck all hurt at once. No matter how I lay, something hurt. I woke myself up from time to time groaning from pain on some pressure point or other. When the alarm went off, I was grateful to get up and leave that night behind.

Roger went out for the newspapers while I made coffee, then I turned on the early television news. There would be no dashing off to school this morning, my routine having been changed by the fall.

At leisure, I glanced at the front page of the St. Louis *Post-Dispatch*, and the previously unsolved murder case was front-page news. A recent color picture of the suspect in orange prison garb stared up at me, and older, black-and-white photos of several more of his now-identified victims were arrayed below. I felt a twinge of sympathy and pity for these women and their families.

I wondered what madness could drive an individual to become a serial killer, preying on women. It seems when we hear stories about these heinous crimes from the media that we are removed from it all, as if it is not quite real and surely not something that will ever impact our own lives.

Yet, there was no denying those pictures were of real, vibrant women, struck down at the whim of a cold, remorseless killer, their lives unfinished, their hopes unfulfilled.

The story continued on page 5. I turned to finish the article. A smaller article beside the conclusion featured a picture of the suspect as he had appeared in the 1970's, his criminal heyday.

I struggled to get my wavy sight focused on the younger person in the photo.

Gobsmacked, yet again.

The jolt of recognition cleared away the fog of the concussion and pain medication instantly. With sudden, stunning clarity, I realized I had seen this man before, in 1978 in my very own neighborhood. His behavior had been so unusual I remembered him. Four days later this individual had returned to our area and brutally murdered a woman who lived two doors away. The police at the time did not seem to have any doubts that I had seen the killer.

I turned to Roger and said, "This is the man that killed Virginia."

I guess Roger's response was logical: How can you be sure? The murder of our neighbor and Roger's co-worker was 29 years ago, and after all, he *was* dealing with a woman with a woozy head injury! And on painkillers, yet! Roger left for work, advising me to take it easy. But I was sure. I had promised myself I would never forget that face.

I re-read the article. I looked at the picture on the front page again. This is how he looks now, I thought. I looked at the older picture again. Yes, I was sure I had seen the man before.

Apparently, a Carbondale, Illinois Detective, Lieutenant Paul Echols, had used DNA evidence to link one Timothy Krajcir to the murder of Southern Illinois University college student Deborah Sheppard. Tragically, she was raped and strangled in 1982, the month before her graduation. Her life was just beginning to take flight and then it was ended abruptly. She was 23 years old.

And, in Cape Girardeau, Missouri, 45 miles away, across the Mississippi River, Detective Jimmy Smith had cold cases of his own. Some similar aspects of crimes he was familiar with seemed to point to Timothy Krajcir, as well. He and Lieutenant Paul Echols began to talk. Other possible victims emerged.

My murdered neighbor was not mentioned in the article. The identified victims were clustered in Cape Girardeau, Missouri, and in Carbondale. Marion was just a 20-minute drive from Carbondale, about 15 miles. I felt there had to be a connection.

A rush of memories brought back that day and time to me. No "story" now, this became all too real; my bruised brain shifted from the present-day story to the past questions and interviews by the police, and to the shell-shocked neighbors reacting to the violence that had erupted among us without warning.

Of course we had hoped a suspect would be identified

quickly. But as the days turned into weeks, heaviness seemed to settle over the neighborhood, and we simply waited.

No news ever came, and this became the coldest of cold cases. It seemed this crime would never be solved. Someone had literally gotten away with murder and could be walking among us every day. People did inquire of the police from time to time for information. As far as I know, we all received the same firm, pat answer, "He's left the area," with no further elaboration.

How the police knew that was a mystery. Where did "he" go? Who was "he"? If "he" was no longer there, why did they not find him, and bring him back to face justice?

A desire for closure runs deeply in all of us. We want to know, at an almost primitive, primal level what happened to people we know or love. We want to know why this terrible thing happened. People feel a need to know so that they can adjust or accommodate their lives in some way to avoid the same fate. The loved ones need to know so they do not have merely the empty chair at the table, the empty side of the bed, the hollow holiday, but can begin to put the trauma behind them and hold onto the happy, warm, living memories of those they cared about.

We needed answers if we were to have this closure. Without this, we simply must settle for burying this terrible happenstance as far in the backs of our minds as possible to deal with the grief and shock until we can begin to move forward.

When violent crime unexpectedly rears its ugly head and looks in your direction, you cannot ever entirely forget. It can come back in a flash; it is as real and raw as the day it happened. All it takes is a memory, a news story, or—a picture.

I wondered if police had reviewed the Virginia Witte case. Having left the area twenty years ago, I was momentarily stumped about whom to ask. Not sure where to start, but determined to once again alert authorities that this person could have played a part my neighbor's death, I picked up the telephone. If there was even a small chance of justice, or closure, would it not be worth looking into?

I dialed directory assistance and asked for the Marion, Illinois police department. There an efficient-sounding woman answered the telephone. I did not really know what to say, so plunged right in. I asked her if anyone in the department worked on old cases.

She asked for my name, I replied "Bonney Patterson", and she put me through to a Detective Morrow.

I identified myself to her, but apparently my name had already been put forth. I explained the news media in St. Louis was leading with the story of the cold case murders. I told her I had once lived in Marion, and was a neighbor of the murdered Virginia Witte, and now lived just west of St. Louis County in St. Charles County, Missouri. I asked her outright if anyone was looking at this man as a possible suspect in connection with the Virginia Witte murder. I mentioned the news articles in the morning *St. Louis Post-Dispatch* and the old photo of the suspect as he had appeared in the 1970s.

I finished, nearly out of breath, saying, "I think this is the man that killed Virginia Witte."

Detective Morrow must have been a bit surprised at this telephone call from the blue and onslaught of words. But she recovered nicely and replied, "I have the file here in front of me right now. I was reading a statement you gave when they told me you were on the phone. So I recognized your name. By the way, this is a pretty good statement."

We talked a few minutes about some details of the case that I had covered earlier (much earlier) in a statement and she also mentioned another former neighbor, Connie Clark. Both Connie and I had seen the same individual and had done our best to recall any and all details that might have been of help to the investigation. Connie had even undergone hypnosis and then been given a post-hypnotic suggestion that she would not remember certain events of that day. Both Detective Morrow and I were not sure what, or if, Connie remembered. Detective Morrow expressed some concern as to how she would react to the news when and if it caught up with her. I told her I would try and get in touch with Connie and she could contact the police if she wanted.

Morrow went on to say that the suspect was in prison on other charges. The death penalty was now in play, and in fact, the Prosecuting Attorney in Cape Girardeau, Missouri was ready to proceed. Krajcir offered to confess to other crimes if the death penalty was removed. It was generally felt this would bring closure to some families with members who had died in the intervening years wondering why their loved ones were taken and having never received answers.

"This afternoon I will be sitting down across from him at the Big Muddy Correctional Center and I will see if he will admit to the Witte murder. If he does, we need to notify family members before we can make a public statement. We may need further statements for the formal charges."

I was happy to agree to cooperate in any way that they might require.

The Detective said Krajcir drove around neighborhoods and parking lots to scout out potential victims. He referred to this as "hunting". I felt my scalp prickle. Yes, I had observed first-hand this technique of Krajcir's. I realized that the encounter I had had was indeed with a serial killer "hunting" human prey for his next victim to assault or even to murder.

We finished up the conversation, and just before we hung up, Detective Morrow said, "This is the guy."

Gobsmacked yet again. It was beginning to feel almost cosmic in nature.

Over the next few days, more details appeared in the news. There was even a small mention of Virginia Witte in connection to the murder investigation. As the investigations unfolded, it became painfully obvious that this was a man who had committed many crimes over many years. He was now willing to confess only because he could finally be tied to capital murder cases and be put to death. With this taken off the table, he would make full confessions of his crimes, a few of which lacked any physical evidence.

It was a surreal week. My head probably would have been spinning without the concussion. It was dizzying, in itself, to contemplate that after all these years, we—family, friends, and neighbors, would finally be able to have answers to questions surrounding a terrible crime. Justice, when we had all but given up, hopefully, would yet prevail.

But as events were rapidly coming together, it became all too easy to be sucked into a quagmire of amazing twists and turns spiraling around a decades-old crime, the ensuing police investigation over the course of some thirty years, and the legal and criminal system that dispenses justice—or not.

A story emerged of a prolific, highly organized and brutal criminal who "hunted" victims for his heinous crimes of sex, robbery, degradation, and even murder.

PART ONE

WITNESS TO MURDER

Chapter One

A New Neighborhood

January, 1978, the Move from Centralia, to Marion, Illinois

Bounding out of bed in a weak, early-morning light, I pulled back the curtain. As I had feared, a deep blanket of white already lay on the ground, and it was still snowing. The movers would be here soon. The kids were staying with their grandparents until we got everything in place at the new house, and Roger was already at his new job. He was waiting in Marion, Illinois. I would follow, alone, after the van was loaded.

It was sad to be leaving our little house. It was the first home we had bought. Our daughter, Sarah, was born in a Chicago suburb in November, 1974. We three moved soon after, and our Son, Jeff, or "Jeffy" as everyone called the baby, was born in Centralia, Illinois in March, 1977. We had been a busy and active part of the community and I had enjoyed our stay. Roger worked for an accounting firm in town and had been offered a Chief Financial Officer position with his "favorite client!" when the current CFO announced his retirement. Another move was on.

We had chosen a house in Westernaire Estates, just west of the city limits of the town of Marion, trading in our snug, three-bedroom ranch for a larger, four-bedroom two-story with full basement. It also had a nice fireplace, which seemed like a great idea for this winter weather! Now all I had to do was get there.

I headed out to Interstate 57 and turned south, into the swirling snowstorm.

The snow continued all day. Great, fat, fluffy flakes were whipped this way and that by gusty, cold winds which proved challenging to the movers. We were all relieved when they gathered their things and departed.

Tiredly, I hoped our new life in a new town, and new house, would be happy and not as ominous as this terrible winter weather seemed to indicate.

Winter had us in its grip and did not want to let go. We bustled around in our new house, unpacking, enjoying the extra space we now had. Sarah loved running up and down the stairs, and like the two-and-a-half-year-old she was, never seemed to lack energy. One day I noticed her sitting on the stairs gazing at her reflection in the mirror hung in the hallway. I asked her what she was doing, and she said, smiling at her "twin" in the mirror, "I like this house—it's just my size!" I laughed and said that this was a big house and she was just a little bitty girl! She giggled.

The new house was vacant when we bought it, and needed some cleaning and a few updates on paint and wallpaper. It was a traditional center hall floor plan downstairs with four bedrooms upstairs. There was a big walk-in closet at the back of our bedroom and the bathroom was to the right. A window in our bath overlooked the railroad tracks and empty field beyond. As privacy did not seem to be an issue, I hung some sheer Priscilla curtains in there. Sarah's bedroom was at the back of the house, Jeff's on the front, and a small bedroom in the middle. There was a lot of light in each room, and three of the bedrooms, including the Master bedroom, had windows overlooking the front yard.

Possibly because we had moved into the neighborhood in the dead of winter, people were tucked away in their homes. I did meet a couple of people right away. One house over, on the opposite corner of Lakeview and Skyline Drive were the Clarks. They had two children, just our kids ages—the older child a girl, and the younger a boy. I hoped they would be good playmates. Connie was for the moment a stay-at-home Mom, as was I. Her husband was a teacher.

On our side of the street, the second house down, perched on that same corner as the Clarks, lived the Wittes, Virginia and David. Virginia, a friendly person, was just about the first new neighbor to come and say hello. She worked for Diagraph Corporation, where Roger was the new CFO, and also in the accounting department. When the wintery weather continued, Roger stopped a few times at the corner to pick Virginia up for work. He joked that he will do just about anything to get his department there in bad weather!

Virginia was a lovely lady in her early fifties, bright and alert and friendly with dark hair and a petite frame. I knew we were both looking forward to better weather. She talked about the new little deck off their breakfast room, and how they couldn't wait to use it. She loved to paint, and this is a perfect spot. They dangled a brightly painted red box with four little "window panes" on a couple of chains from the top of the deck to "frame the view." A bit of whimsy, I thought, for people who enjoy being outside and take pride in their home. I wondered how long she would continue to work, as her husband had retired and they had a first grandbaby on the way, out in Colorado. It seemed to me she has a lot to look forward to besides working.

Finally winter eased. March passed. Baby Jeffy was now a one-year-old. April, and Roger became an old man of 28. Finally, May arrived and we discovered our front yard possessed a thriving crop of dandelions, and some not very lush-looking grass.

I had joined a women's gym, working out during the winter months. I am as "buff" as I ever will be, and in shape to tackle some outdoor projects. Roger started with the sparse grass and prolific dandelions. He put fertilizer on the rather anemic grass, which then finished dying off. He was very annoyed when he caught Sarah joyfully blowing dandelion seed heads in the wind, waving the stalks about as a fairy princess might wave a magic wand. I tackled a planting area at the front of the property on the very east corner, just beside the road. It had been somewhat neglected, but has a nice Birch tree, and a couple of other nice plantings, rocks, etc. I thought with a little trimming, weeding, edging and flowers, it might look very nice.

As the weather steadily improved, I enjoyed working outside in the front yard, as people walked, jogged, or drove by. Most of the time, they waved, or stopped. The road was gravel and oil, leaving loose gravel alongside the grass. It made it easy to hear if someone is coming, either walking or driving along the shoulder, by giving off little crunches under shoes or a crunch-pop from underneath car tires. I always looked up and smiled or waved. After a long winter in a new place, I am happy to meet and greet anyone with a friendly face! I know few people in the subdivision as yet.

Because the kids were little, they still had an afternoon nap after lunch. I tried to get to the gym and run an errand or so in the morning and be home by lunchtime. One day I took the kids to pick out some flowers to put in the planting area I had been working on in the front yard. We find some marigolds that have a bright burst of color. I tell them we will plant them together in the next couple of days.

Chapter Two

Confrontation with a Killer

With Mother's Day coming up, I want to finish the front landscaping, get the house cleaned, and have a cook-out on the weekend. Monday morning I decide to tackle a few errands, and then do my flower planting, getting the bigger chores out of the way first.

After I put the lunch things away, I get out my gardening tools. I have to loosen the soil, so I grab my hand rake and trowel to take to the front yard. Sarah helps to carry the flowers.

Jeffy is going to need his nap soon. He toddles out to the yard in his sister's wake, his feet heavy, and then he plops down in the grass like a dumped sack of flour. I was going to let them help me plant the Marigolds, but I think as I kneel on the ground that I should get them planted quickly, before the kids start fussing. I am careful to position them to my left, toward the house and away from the road, and where I can keep an eye on them. The road is parallel to my right.

It is so lovely to be outdoors. The air is fresh and clean, the breeze soft, the sunshine welcoming. A few people are out and about, some walking, biking. A couple of people drive by and slow down, either because they see little ones out front and are cautious, or to say hello or wave. I am on my hands and knees, busy with the flower planting when I hear a car slowly approaching from behind me. I can hear the loose gravel crunching.

I think, "They are driving on the wrong side of the road", and then the car stops just beside me, to my right. Assuming the driver is stopping to speak to me, I drop back onto my haunches and look up over my shoulder with a smile on my face. I do not wave, as I have gardening tools in each hand.

The road is somewhat elevated, but I can clearly see the person's face, shoulders and the top of the front seat. The crown of his head is somewhat shadowed in the car, but his hair that I can see is dark, as is his mustache and sideburns.

The man in the car stares down hard at me. He does not blink and does not speak. My smile fades. I have not seen him before and he seems anything but friendly. I do not understand the intensity I feel from him. Feeling a glimmer of unease, not yet alarmed, I turn to more fully face him, still in my kneeling position.

I can feel the warm sunshine caressing the crown of my head, but strangely, at the same time, I feel coldness and my hair prickles on the back of my neck. My hands reflexively grip my gardening tools, and I quickly glance down, just to be sure I have them.

I look back up at this man, trying to puzzle out what he might want, or why he is here. The car is sideways so I am not sure exactly which model of car it is, but I note color, type of seats. I note the lack of pinstriping on the exterior, or dents or dings; the vehicle seems shiny and new. His right arm does not extend over the top of the seat; he is probably using this hand to hold the steering wheel. He is partially turned towards me, his left shoulder dipping somewhat and I think either he has something in his left hand, or it is possibly on the door handle, or his elbow is on the armrest. He does not lean out of the window, which is rolled completely down, as he would if he wanted to greet me, but stays as much as possible within the shadow of the car. Parked maybe ten feet, or less, away from where I am kneeling with my newly planted flowers, he seems unhurried, intent, and I study him.

Basically, I see a neat, nice-looking man, well-groomed, broad shoulders, in his late 20s or early 30s with dark hair. His hair is perfectly in place and his eyes are staring unwaveringly at me. In this small town I live in, where doors are not always

16

locked, had he approached me in a different, friendlier manner, asked for directions, or asked to use the telephone, I might have gotten up and gone over to his car, or even let him in the house to use my phone.

Uneasy now, I steal a quick glance behind me, to check on my babies. Sarah is dancing across the lawn while scattering dandelion seeds. Jeffy has slumped into a semi-sitting position on the grass, still with thumb in mouth, chin on his chest, nearly asleep sitting up. A small, brief sliver of recognition quickly flits through my mind that I am the only one, so far, to notice this man. That the children are not paying any attention brings faint relief. I do not want them frightened or coming any closer to the road.

I suddenly have a visual flash of what this man is seeing; the house, the young mother planting flowers, the small children. I am thankful they are both behind me but I know if this stranger gets out of his car he will not look quite so neat in short order. He has to come through me for whatever he wants, and I involuntarily grip my gardening tools tighter. I do not consider, for some reason, that this might be a case of unwarranted hysterics.

My mind has begun to whir at an incredible speed. I play several scenarios in my head very, very quickly. I want to jump up and grab the kids and run into the house. Do I want to put the gardening tools down? Then I have no defenses. Can I pick up both children and run into the house and lock the door fast enough? Can I hope to outrun him carrying two little ones? Probably not. And I will have to put one child down to open the front door.

The thought of putting one of my children down with possible danger lurking at my back makes ice water run through my veins. I feel that coldness spread throughout my body. I wonder if Sarah could run to a neighbor's house, and whether the risk that this stranger could push or follow us into the house was too great to even try to get in the door. What would happen to us behind a closed door? So, what does that leave me?

With a flight-or-fight adrenalin surge in full force, I tell myself to stay put—outside. Anyone could come by and if he were going to make a move, he would have done it by now. My heart is racing and he continues staring at me. So I stare back, with my children behind me, my garden tools in my hands.

It appears to be a draw. If he wants to frighten or intimidate me, he has. But I cannot go anywhere, not now.

Finally, he looks beyond me, and looks hard at Sarah, then at Jeffy, and then back to me. He wants to see if I am paying attention. Then he glances at each of the upper three bedroom windows, nodding, as if he is counting, one, two, three. He looks back down at me, then at each child. Was he somehow threatening me? He then put his car in drive. At the intersection of Lakeview and Westernaire Drive, only a couple of houses away, I see his brake lights go on. He has stopped again. I wait, still on my knees, garden tools in hand, not yet willing to give up my position. I watch as this rather ominous stranger looks up at the street signs, and then turns right at the corner, and is finally out of sight.

I immediately scoop up the baby, snare Sarah under one arm, relief flooding through me as I run to the house. I lock everything on the first floor that can be locked. After I tuck the kids in for naps, they fall asleep quickly, safe and sound in their own little beds. I check several times on Sarah and Jeff as they lay napping. They look so very sweet and innocent. The adrenaline has faded, leaving me with the shakes. I circled the downstairs more than once, double-checking that all locks were engaged.

I try very hard over the next few hours to convince myself this was just some weird person, or someone having a very bad day and trying to take it out on whomever. Maybe he lived nearby, and was not very friendly, or did not like children? Maybe he was just looking for someone in the neighborhood, or cutting through. I knew of no laws he had broken to report to the police. His behavior was certainly out-of-the-ordinary, and he had given me some bad moments of extreme unease, which burned the memory into my brain. I filed it away, just in case I ever encountered him again, and told myself to forget about it for now. I certainly did not expect to ever see or hear from him again. Everything was all right, after all. The kids were napping and no one was breaking into the house through my doors or windows. All was as it should be. Probably I was just being silly. It was an overreaction; what else could it be?

Friday morning the kids and I were out and about. I thought I might carve out some time to go to my gym before I made the kids their lunch, so I decided to swing by the house and pick up my gym bag. I wished I had had the foresight to put the bag into the car before I left. It was sitting in the floor of my walk-in-closet. Time was going to be tight, and I might have to do a 45-minute workout in 30! It was already close to 12 noon.

I pulled onto Skyline and approached the corner of Lakeview. I had noticed signs of activity at Virginia's house. She and her husband apparently had just returned from their vacation. The shades were up, a few of their windows open. I thought their plans were not to come home for another day or two, something she had mentioned while still at work. The anticipated grandbaby out in Colorado had arrived, and then their son had won a trip for himself and his wife soon after. Perfect timing for eager new grandparents to baby-sit! But possibly this was David Witte's day to meet his retired buddies for lunch, so maybe they came home early. I knew Virginia would be up and bustling about, probably airing out the house and running errands.

I looked forward to seeing more of Virginia in the neighborhood; she had left her full-time job at Diagraph just before they went on their vacation. She had not worked long enough to have accrued vacation time and wanted to go, badly. I would have to go over as soon as I saw her and inquire about her trip and that new grandbaby!

The corner was a hive of activity—Connie Clark, just across the street from the Wittes, had her lawn mower fired up. The Clark's corner lot was small, a postage-stamp-sized patch of grass. But Connie would mow with a will, and finish up fairly quickly. She had a system, I had noticed. She would mow one area, then the next. Apparently the back was already done, as she was mowing the front corner closest to my house. Her daughter, Heidi, was playing outside with a couple of other little girls in the driveway, away from the area her Mom was mowing. Connie would be done with her yard pretty soon! I do not see the silver-colored car that has passed Connie's house, making her uneasy.

I was in a hurry. Pulling partway into my driveway, I jumped out of my car, leaving the kids seat belted in their car seats in the back. I left the car in the driveway, with the driver's door wide open. I ran into the back door, also leaving it wide open. I ran up the stairs, stepped into my walk-in closet, grabbed my gym bag, and turned to run back down the stairs and to the car.

In one fairly fluid motion, I take my keys out of my pocket, throw the bag into the passenger seat, slide behind the steering wheel, then close the door. As I put the car in reverse, I turn and grin at Sarah and Jeffy. They grin back. I feel my spirits lift. It has been a busy day, so far, but the weather is great, the kids are happy, and all in all, it is a great day to be alive.

Backing down the driveway, we headed off in the other direction, toward town, leaving Lakeview and Skyline behind in my rear view mirror.

I finished up at the gym in pretty good time, getting back home a little before one o'clock. After a quick lunch, I took Sarah and Jeffy upstairs and tucked them in for their naps, returned to tidy the kitchen, and then wandered outside, across the street, to pick up my mail. Connie has apparently finished mowing, all is quiet, the kids have gone indoors, and her yard looks nice.

As I stood beside the mailbox on the opposite side of the road, reading and sorting my mail, I glanced toward Virginia's house. The front bedroom shades were down and the windows shut. Virginia liked fresh air to circulate and didn't she earlier have the house airing out after their nearly two-week trip? Usually the window shades were up, at least. Hadn't they been up before? Odd how quiet it seemed. I thought briefly about knocking on her door to inquire about their trip, but decided maybe later. Perhaps they were tired from their trip and taking an early, after-lunch afternoon siesta. From my vantage point I was unable to observe if Virginia's car or anyone else's was then parked in her driveway. But something seemed not quite right.

Frowning slightly, I went back inside with my mail.

About ten minutes later, someone knocked on my front door. I opened it to find a uniformed police officer. He asked me if I had seen any suspicious people in the neighborhood that day. It was the first question of many others to follow. I said, "No, why? Has there been a break-in?"

"No, ma'am," came the reply. "A homicide."

Many years later, we would all still be searching for answers.

Chapter Three

Virginia and David Witte

After the initial December, 2007 conversation between Detective Morrow of the Marion police and me, and subsequent conversations later with both her and Lieutenant Echols, it seemed that with everything concerning the confessed murderer, Timothy Krajcir, in his criminal heyday, more questions popped up. Detective Morrow was not always available to answer some of those questions; indeed she may not have had the answers even after hearing Krajcir's fairly detailed confession. Much time has passed and many crimes, besides, for this career criminal. I decided I would look to the case file itself for some answers. During the last couple of weeks in April 2008, I received permission to obtain information from the files that I requested under the Illinois Freedom of Information Act. There were still so many unanswered questions: the most puzzling was how could it even be in the realm of possibility to fall victim to a serial killer? The answer turned out to be that it was, chillingly enough, easy, as well as random.

Information from investigative reports held some surprises for me, but they were pretty matter-of-fact.

According to the case files, the Wittes had just returned in the early evening hours the Thursday night before from their trip to Colorado.

Mr. Witte had worked as a General Motors representative in Marion, Illinois prior to 1969 but then transferred to Kansas City. There he suffered a heart attack and retired on a pension.

The Wittes felt they would have a cheaper and better quality of life by moving back once again to the Marion area. They knew people there and in nearby St. Louis and had previously lived close by the house they eventually purchased on the corner of Lakeview and Skyline Drive. Only a year was to pass before Virginia was murdered.

Mr. Witte was a veteran of World War II and did some volunteer work at the Veteran's Administration Hospital in Marion until his elderly father was admitted there for treatment. Virginia and David Witte had taken his father in for an unspecified duration of time. He did not live long thereafter, and David Witte became upset with the care his father received at the VA. His volunteer activities there ceased.

Next Mr. Witte started a home-based repair business. His ad in the local newspaper generated so *many* calls that he soon quit this altogether. At the time of his wife's murder, he did not have any outside business interests to speak of, but had thoughts of trying out financial management.

Early in 1978 Virginia ventured out to seek employment. Whether she needed some extra money, or insurance, or a break from non-stop "coupledom", or all the above, is unclear. She obtained a position at Diagraph Bradley. Both my husband, who was CFO, and the Corporate Secretary, Grace Dusch, and another lady who worked in the computer department, all lived in the Westernaire subdivision. Perhaps that is why she applied.

She was hired approximately in February of that year.

Dick Stenkenrider, who was the plant superintendent, was interviewed by police that May, 1978. He stated that Virginia had been employed "in the Accounting Department" and that she "was friendly, although most of the time she sort of kept to herself. (She) was well-liked by the other employees. Mrs. Witte was always very neat and well dressed."

He further stated, "The reason Mrs. Witte terminated her employment was because she wished to take a vacation and since she had been employed only approximately two to three months, had no vacation time due her."

Additionally, a statement from a friend of David Witte confirmed she quit her job about a week before leaving for Denver. The friend, who may have been parroting David Witte, told a detective that the work was too hard for her and that she preferred to indulge in her hobby, painting.

The Witttes started driving to Denver, Colorado to babysit for their new granddaughter, as their son had won a trip for himself and his wife from the car dealership he worked for. Another son then lived in Kansas City, a stop along the way. They planned to see friends from the time that they had lived in Kansas City, as well.

They drove their station wagon and were gone nine or ten days, returning about 6 p.m. the evening of Thursday, May 11, 1978.

The next morning, the pantry was bare. They needed groceries. Mr. Witte indicated they had not had any breakfast that day, only some instant coffee. Virginia planned to go to the Kroger store to buy groceries, while Mr. Witte had made plans to go to lunch.

A friend had called the night before and again Friday morning between 8 and 9 a.m. to invite him. Several men were getting together, among them the grandfather of a future Lieutenant of the Carbondale, Illinois Police Department who would eventually provide the break in this case as well as others.

When the friend arrived to pick up David Witte, Virginia had already left in the station wagon.

Virginia must have been a little hungry. The toxicology lab report showed she had some food in her stomach, ingested about two hours before death, and identified as popcorn or some type of cereal. She may have picked up a snack at her house from the pantry, or maybe she had stopped along the way for something.

The Kroger store tape suggests she checked out at the register about 11:30 a.m. She also stopped to purchase a $.69 item from Big Star shortly after leaving Kroger, on her way home.

It would only have taken ten minutes, at the most, to drive home from there. She probably arrived at her house around 11:40 to 11:50 a.m.

Connie was out mowing her front yard. They waved.

Virginia parked the station wagon in the driveway and began

taking the groceries in through the garage and into the adjoining kitchen. The garage door was left open to better facilitate her moving the groceries from the car and into the kitchen.

David Witte and his friend, a Mr. Ford, returned from their luncheon around 1 p.m. He pulled his car into the driveway and parked beside the station wagon. He did not mention seeing anything amiss, such as an open door on the car, or groceries still inside the car, or the garage door being open. Perhaps all was as it should have been.

David Witte said good-bye to his friend in the driveway and Mr. Ford did not go into the house, as he did when he picked Mr. Witte up earlier.

Mr. Ford tried to start his brown Cadillac Seville, but he had some difficulty. He stated he "had trouble starting the Seville at the Witte house."

He further stated he was not able to return to his home until 15 or 20 minutes after that 1 p.m. drop-off time.

Per a MapQuest of the area, Mr. Ford only had to go south on Skyline Drive to Old Route 13 (a couple of blocks), turn past the VA hospital and go about three more blocks. This is ten minutes, tops.

Where was David Witte for that approximately ten minutes? Was he standing in the driveway with his friend as he struggled to get his car started? Neither one gave a statement about this happenstance. Did David turn away and go inside his house? No statement says that, either.

His friend having departed, perhaps David Witte then walked into his house via the garage and into the kitchen.

He would have immediately noticed groceries on the counter and packages of carrots and chicken in the sink, as well as Virginia's purse, which was knocked off the counter and all the contents spilled out onto the floor. He would have noticed some blood on the dishwasher panel to his left, just inside the door, and spots of blood on the kitchen floor.

Perhaps puzzled by the disarray there, he then walked into the great room, past the dining room, calling Virginia's name, turning to his left, down the hall, stopping when he saw blood in the hall bath, and continued on down the hall to the Master bedroom where Virginia lay sprawled on the bed, naked, strangled, her abdomen slashed open and with a knife protruding from her chest.

We can imagine him backpedaling out of the room, going into another room to use the telephone to call police, then blindly rushing out of what had become his house of horrors, across the street to summon help, to talk to someone, to have someone wait with him until somebody, somehow arrived to make sense of what his mind could not grasp, could not process.

Sadly, there was no help available that could put things right or give David Witte the answers he surely wanted. He would pass on before the murder of his wife would be solved.

Chapter Four

Murder in Marion

May 12, 1978

This delightful spring day started out like every other day. Moms fixing breakfast, doing some housekeeping chores, lunch, putting the baby down for a nap. Little Heidi Clark, who was not one to nap very often, went outside with her Mom. Connie wanted to finish mowing the yard. Her husband had mowed in the back of the house last evening. While little brother Jon was down for his nap was a good time to finish the rest of the lawn. Heidi attracted a couple of other little girls. They settled down to play in the driveway while her Mom mowed.

Connie started mowing on the east end of the house. It was not a large area to mow, but after finishing that section she started on the front. The mower began giving her some trouble. Connie stopped to fiddle with it in the front, northeastern corner. She was keeping an eye on the girls playing in the driveway.

She noticed a strange man driving slowly by in a silver-colored car. His window was half-down. He was coming from the east on Lakeview, passing the Patterson house on the right and heading toward the intersection. He was staring intently. He stopped at the corner and looked at her daughter, Heidi, and the other little girls playing in the driveway. Then he drove away, turning left, or south, on Skyline Drive. Connie was uneasy with this man and had not seen him before.

Connie got the mower started again. She wanted to finish the front yard and the ditch area. As she began mowing, once again the stranger passed slowly by the house. He had come from the same direction. She had the impression he was looking for someone.

Once more, he stared at her and then at the girls playing. He left the same way as before. He did not speak to her or the girls or ask directions or for anyone in particular. Connie did not like him being close to the children, and called them away from the road.

The night before, Connie had observed that Virginia Witte and her husband, David, had come back from their vacation. She noticed some activity over at their house just across the road about 6 or 7 p.m.

Virginia had apparently just returned from the grocery store. She had pulled her car into the driveway and taken a couple of bags of groceries into the house through the garage. The garage door was left open. The kitchen is immediately accessible through the garage.

Even though the Wittes and the Clarks live directly across the street from each other they did not socialize much. The Wittes had an older set of friends. David was retired; Virginia was until recently working full-time, as she was only in her early 50s. The Clarks had not been in the Witte house, but Connie volunteered to water plants that Virginia set out on the front porch while they were gone. Virginia usually honked or waved when she passed by if the Clarks were outside. She seemed like a friendly person.

Connie, nearly finished mowing, was thinking how good a shower would feel!

"Oh no," she thinks. She had seen that man coming back, this time driving due north on Skyline. He stopped at the corner of Virginia's house, just shy of her driveway. The strange man got out of the car, and then placed his hands on the car and looked all around, in every direction, up and down Lakeview and Skyline. He was apparently looking for someone, but there was Virginia right in front of him, busily removing her groceries from her car. She went into the house, and the man got quickly back into his car, pulled into the driveway, and parked alongside Virginia's station wagon. Connie watched all this maneuvering by this unknown man as she finished up her lawn mowing, then thought that everything must have been all right, as it seemed he was just visiting the Wittes. Maybe he had been circling the block waiting for one of them to come home. He went through the garage and into the house very quickly, as if he knew exactly what he was doing and what he came for.

She noted, however, that Virginia did not speak to the man, or wave to him. She apparently did not pay much attention to him at all.

Connie did not see it, but he was carrying a box. He knocked at the back door and when Virginia opened it, pretended to have a package for her to sign for. He had made it into the house.

Virginia will not get all her groceries put away.

Connie was nearly finished mowing now. Along came the Witte dog, a beautiful boxer. He ran up to Connie and the children, circling and barking. He seemed excited, and Connie tried to shoo him back across the street. "What is wrong with this stupid dog?" Connie thought.

She gathered up Heidi and friends and headed into the house. That shower was next on her agenda.

Someone pounded at the front door. The shower was cut short. She told the girls to say to whomever it was, "Just a minute", while she hurried to get dressed. She went to see who was knocking so urgently.

It was David Witte. He asked her to step outside, where the girls couldn't hear.

What he said to her is unbelievable. Virginia had been *murdered*. He said he found her dead and called the police from his house. He said he was very careful not to touch anything.

Connie thought, "Oh no, oh no, oh no." She thought she should have called the police when she saw that man. She asked David Witte if he was all right. She wanted to go in and see if Virginia was actually dead, as she feared she might be in need of assistance. Apparently she has no doubts as to the person who must have committed the crime.

She also was thinking, "Thank God he didn't get the girls." And, "Lock the doors."

Connie cannot believe Virginia is dead.

"No," David Witte said, "she's dead."

They moved over to his front yard, waiting for the police to arrive. They did not go into the house, and the garage door was then closed. The anticipated arrival of the police seemed to take forever.

Connie went back home to call the police again. She also called the Fire Department. She then waited with David Witte in his front yard until the police came and asked her to go back to her house and wait for someone to come and take a statement from her.

Ironically, the first emergency vehicle to respond was the ambulance. It sat in the driveway for a long time. Eventually it took her body away. It seemed like an eternity before police arrived.

When they did get there, they must have been shocked and unprepared for what they found.

The police began canvassing the neighborhood right away, knocking on doors; they asked people if they had seen anyone suspicious that day. Since the Witte house was on the corner, it was easily accessible from both old and new Route 13, and Interstate 57 as well as Route 148. It could have been anybody coming or going from several directions who had committed the crime.

However, several people had seen the silver-colored car, some had seen the man driving the vehicle, and some had seen the car parked in the driveway.

A second-grade teacher who lived in the subdivision was taking her class on a field trip, riding the small, old-fashioned locomotive that ran on the tracks behind the houses on the north side of Lakeview. It was more of a tourist attraction than anything else, gaily painted, with a cowcatcher and billowing smoke, and the kids loved to wave at it as it chugged by a few times a week. She noticed the silver car in the driveway as the little train passed by the house.

Because Connie had seen the man who had gone into the Witte house, the police were very interested in talking to her. They wanted help in a couple of areas. First, they wanted her help in drawing a sketch of this man. They also wanted to further pinpoint the vehicle, and figured the license plate or a partial number on a plate would be good information.

Eventually they asked her to undergo hypnosis to try to recover any memories she might have regarding the license plate. Because she had seen the car about three times she thought maybe she could get this information for them.

Chapter Five

The Investigation Begins

At 1:35 p.m. Detectives Woolsey and Odom went to talk to Connie. She gave a timeline, reporting that she had gone outside to mow at 11:30 a.m. She began on the east side of the house, getting to the front yard at approximately noon.

The report states that she was "mowing on the Northeast side of the residence approximately 10 to 15 feet from the roadway when a Silver colored vehicle approached going west bound on Lakeview. (She stated) that the vehicle slowed down; the driver's window was part of the way down and she thought the man in the car was either looking for someone or he was going to stop and ask her a question. The subject turned his head; looking at some children who were playing in her yard. Mrs. Clark states that his actions bothered her and as he drove past, turning onto Skyline Drive proceeding southbound, she called the children and had them come into the yard away from the street. Mrs. Clark continued to mow and within a few minutes the same vehicle approached again from the east; going west on Lakeview. The subject (again) turning south on Skyline Drive."

They then asked her to describe the car, which she did, describing a new silver car, "possibly a Chevrolet."

They asked her to describe the individual, and she stated he was approximately 35, "possibly heavy set, rounded face, dark framed glasses (Krajcir later said he was probably wearing sunglasses), long side burns to the bottom of the ears, dark brown or black hair very neatly groomed."

She described his clothing as well.

By 2:00 p.m. Woolsey had telephoned the Illinois State Police in DuQuoin, Illinois and requested that they broadcast information on both vehicle and person of interest.

Woolsey and Odom then welcomed a third Detective, by the name of Henshaw, and another policeman, Captain Carl Kirk, was sent for to come to the residence and make a composite sketch of the suspect.

Connie then was asked to continue the interview by picking up the timeline. She stated "that after the silver car passed the second time and again turned south on Skyline Drive....within a few minutes the silver colored car returned; this time from the south on Skyline Drive going north. The car passed and pulled into the Witte's driveway."

"Mrs. Clark states she felt differently about the car after it had parked in the Witte's driveway as she felt then that the man had just been looking for them."

In another interview on the next day, she volunteered that at "approximately noon, or just before, Clark states that she looked and that the (silver colored) car was parked on the street on Skyline Drive, by Witte's driveway, facing north. Clark further stated that by the angle, she could not tell if Virginia Witte's car was in her drive way."

She finished mowing, went into the house and looked at the clock. It was 1:07 p.m., and she indicated the clock was a couple or three minutes fast.

Time was running out for her neighbor across the street.

The Detectives asked her if she "could recall the approximate time that (David) Witte had come to her house, and she stated that she believed it to be between 1:12 and 1:15 p.m."

"David Witte told Clark, 'We have a problem. Ginny has been murdered. I didn't touch anything,' and asked if she had seen anything. Witte stated that he had called the police from his home. Clark went ahead and called by telephone the Fire Department and then the City Police."

"Clark then went with David Witte back over to the Witte's yard. She did not go into the Witte house. The Witte garage door was shut."

I was able to obtain a transcript of the interview that Connie gave under hypnosis. This took place on August 8, 1978, and lasted 33 minutes.

At the end of the interview, she was given a suggestion that she would not remember certain things. I too had been asked to consider undergoing hypnosis. I thought about it, but in the end, I said no. I simply thought I had given them all the information I had. I knew I had never seen the license plate, which they were so keenly pursuing. Mainly, I had seen the side of the car, and when he pulled away, the lower bumper area was obscured by the bush in the planting area I was working in. I was certainly eager to be of any assistance in any way possible, but I did not think I had anything more to add to the investigation.

And, as I said to Connie at the time, "Forget it? No, if I see this guy coming, I want to know him and run the other way!"

A couple of things stared out at me from the hypnosis transcript. Connie did not remember, if you had asked her, that she saw the stranger's car leave. She stated here, though, that "he left the house fast. He was in the house a long time. 40 minutes. He hit (the railroad) tracks so fast. Hit hi(s) brakes. Was he surprised."

In a statement dated May 12 and conducted by a Detective Woolsey, she says she "did not observe the subject getting out of the car nor did she see the car leave." Was this something that the hypnosis pulled, some forgotten detail in a statement given on the very day of the murder?

And, "That brown car. Just missed your company." David Witte was dropped off after his luncheon with his friends. By someone with a brown car, the friend Mr. Ford. Apparently, they missed Krajcir by just a hair, probably about five minutes.

Also, she states "I could have saved her" while under hypnosis. To this day, she says that if she had just taken the dog back across the street, maybe knocked on the door, she "could have saved her."

And I maintain that if she had done so, she might have been pulled into that house and been a victim, too.

Even though her suspicions were aroused by the actions of this man, as were mine, he had broken no laws by driving down the street. What could have been reported? Would the police even have taken this seriously? Or would they have dismissed us as flighty housewives seeing potential rapists or murderers behind every bush?

I obtained two additional transcripts of statements made by Connie. In a short span of time, they asked her about everything they could think of.

The other thing that I note from all the transcripts is the lack of concrete information she was able to provide about the license plate. They pressed her for information on the plate. She was not sure it was even one issued in Illinois. It turns out it was, indeed an Illinois plate. Not only that, but it had part of the killer's initials followed by random numbers.

She tried really hard, but could not give them information she did not have.

The Investigative Memorandum dated 5-12-78 from Wesley C. Swafford, Marion Police Department begins with a puzzling call from the radio operator at 1:10 p.m.

He and his partner, Sergeant Jack West, were dispatched to the Lakeview address of the Witte house with the cryptic message that they "would understand when.....(they) arrived."

Arrive they did, at 1:15 p.m., parking behind an ambulance. Standing beside the ambulance was the driver. Connie Clark was in the front yard talking to David Witte.

The two policemen started toward the house and then Mr. Witte intercepted them, saying, "There had been a murder. Don't touch anything."

Swafford requested everyone stay outside, but Mr. Witte continued on inside the house, again stating, "I haven't touched anything. Don't touch anything."

As they entered the kitchen, Swafford "noticed an open drawer to my left, (just inside the door) and a purse on the floor with its contents scattered about, and groceries on the cabinet top."

He wrote, "Myself, Mr. Witte and Sgt. West went through the kitchen, a dining area, and into a family room. I again requested that Mr. Witte go back outside. Witte then stated, 'Through that door and left, down the hall.' Mr. Witte then went back toward the kitchen and outside."

The two officers went down the hallway towards the Master

bedroom, meeting an EMT from the ambulance service.

"He said that she was dead."

They passed the hall bath and saw the light was on but did not notice anything else then.

Entering the bedroom they saw a nude female lying on her back on the bed. It appeared that she had sat down on the edge of the bed and had fallen backwards from that position. Her sandals were still on her feet.

"The upper abdomen had been opened and a knife was protruding from the upper left of the chest area below the breast. There was a butcher-type knife lying on a chair to the right of the bedroom door. Above and to the right of the victim's head was a white, bloody cloth. In her left hand was a white, bloody cloth, and a brassiere was lying on the left side of the body…..some clothing lying in the floor beside the bed."

The officers then proceeded to search the house, beginning with the small bath off the Master bedroom but found no one hiding in the house.

They then moved outside to secure the area.

Mr. Witte was asked if he needed anyone like a doctor, pastor, relative or anyone else called.

His response was, "No one and that his only medical problem was that his mouth was dry."

They noted Connie's name and address and asked her to go home to be interviewed.

Swafford and West were relieved by Detectives Wiseman of the Williamson County Detective Unit and Detective Henshaw of the Williamson County Sheriff's Office.

The knives were identified as being part of a set of knives owned by the Wittes and kept in that open drawer by the back door as noted by the police upon entering the house.

In that hallway bathroom with the light still on, blood stains were found. The door of the cabinet under the sink, where the towels were stored, was open. These were photographed.

Also, the medicine cabinet door was open and on top of the vanity sink area was a box of band-aids, open, and one band-aid wrapper. These were also photographed.

Virginia was found clutching a wash cloth in the hand and under the wash cloth was a "band aid between the thumb and finger."

According to a conversation I had with Detective Morrow, this was where a struggle for the knife must have taken place. Virginia was forced to climb up on to the stool lid at knife point, most likely having removed her lower clothing.

Possibly she had just been forced to give Krajcir oral sex in the front bedroom, the one she may have used as her own room.

At this point, she decided to fight back.

In desperation, as he held the knife on her while living yet another of his sexual fantasies, she grabbed the knife blade in her bare hand. He let it go, but before she could turn it around and put the knife to use against him, he quickly snatched it out of her hand, cutting the webbing between her thumb and pointer finger.

It bled profusely, thus the band-aid which she requested he allow her to get. When that proved insufficient, the towel and wash cloth were also used to try to stanch the blood flow. This probably also accounted for the large amounts of blood found on her blouse. She may have cradled her injured hand to her chest while wrapped in the towel/washcloth as she was forced down the hall toward the master bedroom.

There was blood on the edges of the sink—someone had wiped this and left a bloody residue, according to the report by Officer Swafford.

Also, in the sink itself "was a drop of blood that had run down and the metal stopper in the sink had blood in it. It was wet so we let it dry, so we removed the trap from the sink (and sent it to the lab to determine) if this was Mrs. Witte's blood or someone else's."

The police and Mr. Witte determined that nothing at all was taken. $10,000 worth of diamond rings were either on Virginia's fingers or on top of the dresser; her wallet was lying on the kitchen floor with the money still there; and she was wearing a gold chain with a pearl on it around her neck at the time of her death.

They were also struck by the lack of signs of struggle—they looked at a mark on one wall, but Mr. Witte thought that had been there before.

During an earlier conversation I had with a Mr. Steven Swofford, an attorney (I will quote him later in this book), one thing he said popped into my mind as I reviewed this material.

He had stated that he liked to get as close as he could to his victims so he could easily overpower them and they could not get away. Gentleness was not one of the killer's qualities. He liked to use brute force quickly and overwhelm his victims before they quite realized what was happening and had a chance to fight back or try to escape.

It is highly possible that Krajcir dropped the pretense of delivering a package as soon as he stepped through that door. It is also possible he used a choke-hold on Virginia as well as holding a knife on her. He may well have had his buck knife with him that day. Somehow, blood was drawn right there in the kitchen after he entered the house. Not a lot, but enough to possibly further intimidate or shock Virginia and impress upon her he was not a man who could be denied or defied. He did not want to kill her then. He had a fantasy of rape and murder in his head and an overpowering compulsion to live it out. He needed a somewhat willing, preferably frightened partner to make it all come true.

This would fit the coroner's report that broken blood vessels in her neck could have been caused by this type of injury from the choke-hold, above and beyond the bruising from the strangulation.

It might also account for the lack of struggle throughout the house—from the moment he stepped through the door he had control over his victim. The only time she was able to defy him and fight back was when she grabbed the knife in the bathroom.

One other item I discovered in the Case Files that day was a press release from the Williamson County Detective Unit date 6-28-78 which stated:

"The body also had numerous puncture wounds apparently made by a round, sharp object that left residue such as lead, ink, or other unknown substance."

A wine corkscrew was taken from the Witte home, but was tested and was clean.

Mr. Witte was asked if he owned an ice pick, but he said no, and none was found at the house.

The bloody blouse found beside the body on the bed was thought to have puncture holes in it corresponding to those that were found on the body, but when it was carefully examined at the FBI lab, it was found to be free of holes.

There is a letter from a private lab in the case files addressing a section of injured skin that was removed at autopsy, frozen and sent for further study. The lab could not determine the object that caused the wounds or the substance around the wound.

The statement of 6-28-78 also clearly stated, "The victim was not sexually assaulted as determined by the pathologist." At least no semen was found in the vaginal area, possibly having been previously expended through forced oral sex.

I attempted to gain clarification on this from Detective Christina Morrow, and she said she had no problem with the lack of semen. In his confession, Krajcir indicated that "then we had sex."

"As if," Detective Morrow said, "this had been consensual sex and not at knifepoint."

I had always hoped and prayed Virginia was no longer alive when he slashed her upper abdomen open and stabbed her with the knife. It was generally known, at the time, that she was both strangled and also stabbed. This seemed so senseless, so brutal, that the question "Why?" hung suspended over the crime for me and others for years and years. And we still do not have the answer to that question. Perhaps Krajcir himself does not have the answer to that question.

During his confession, according to Detective Morrow, Krajcir said he strangled her for 4 or 5 minutes. Her body was convulsing, and he did not know if she was actually dead or not. He decided to be sure he was leaving no witness to identify him. He went to the kitchen and found some household knives in a drawer by the back door. The butcher-type knife he discarded onto a chair in the bedroom. It proved too dull. Krajcir made, as noted in the autopsy report, "numerous" jabs in her chest. Thus, the puncture wounds and surrounding bruises as noted in the autopsy report. But Krajcir did not intend to just puncture. He was in a killing frenzy; he compulsively needed to stab and mutilate. Tossing this knife on the chair, he then went back to the kitchen for another knife from the drawer. This knife was better, sharper; it delivered the slash and was then buried in her chest.

There it remained.

The coroner's report, however, with the investigative reports

40

I have read, do indicate some small blood splatter toward the head board and also to one side of the bed. The best conclusion is that the knifing, the slashing and stabbing, was delivered as she lay dying after the strangulation, her heart still beating, but barely. Thus, he slashed and stabbed her body as she was in her death throes. Hoping for a small mercy, we can assume she had lost consciousness.

"You mean someone's been *killed*?" I asked in disbelief.

The policeman's eyes flicked involuntarily towards his left. He asked if I would be available to answer a few questions later.

"Of course. But, who was murdered?"

"The lady on the corner," was his reply.

I thought he could mean Connie or Virginia, so I asked hesitantly, "Do you mean Virginia?"

He nodded.

I went to telephone my husband at work. Virginia had, after all, worked in his department and he and her former co-workers, a couple of whom she was friendly with, would find out something terrible had happened soon enough on the evening news if I did not prepare them.

"Roger, something has happened to Virginia. They say she's been murdered. Maybe there is some mistake. The police just left, and they want to come back later to take some kind of statement."

He decided to come home to find out what was going on. Unsettled, I stepped outside. From my vantage point I could not see the driveway where the ambulance was parked, but there seemed to be some people milling around. The children were upstairs, asleep, and I did not want to leave them, if only for a minute to walk down to the corner.

Passing the Witte house on his way home, Roger confirmed activity at Virginia's house on the corner. He saw the ambulance in the driveway and police cars at their house.

He wandered out the back door and briefly talked to a couple of policemen in the Witte's back yard. I watched the exchange. One of the police officers looked too weak to stand, and the other made a slashing gesture with his hand.

"What's going on?" I asked as he came back inside.

"There are two police officers in their back yard, and they

are sick. They were throwing up. One looks pretty green still. They told me he used a knife."

Not a pretty picture to see two ill policemen. I always kept a pitcher with ice water and usually tea or other beverage in the refrigerator (this was before the days of ice water and ice conveniently available on the door). Taking one of the pitchers and a tray and a couple of glasses I offered it to the officers, who were appreciative. They didn't look a lot better, but I think it helped.

We did not have a cook-out that weekend. We spent some time at the funeral home instead. Also, the police started canvassing the neighborhood. I met with them several times. At first, after the shocking news, I was mainly concentrating on whether I had seen anyone that particular day. Since I had been coming and going, I was not able to give much information. I had literally missed the action, popping in and out, as the murderer circled our block. If I had seen him, I would have recognized him as the man who drove up to my house and stopped that past Monday.

Would that have made a difference? Sadly, probably not. Another sighting would just have made him a more familiar figure to me. I was new in the neighborhood and did not know everybody. If I had seen him leave the Witte residence, I probably would have gone to the house and knocked on the door, though, just to find out who this strange person was. But I stood at my mailbox just after or, possibly just before, Krajcir left the house. It was a short span of time that was crucial, about forty minutes for Krajcir to get into the residence, commit the crimes, and then leave again before Mr. Witte returned home. I saw no one out and about at that time. No friend delivering David Witte back home, no car stalled in the driveway, no one running across the street to Connie's.

It only takes a couple of minutes to drive the described route that Krajcir took around those few short blocks that day. Recently I drove this just to time it. Partly curious as to my own timing that day, I concluded that I either went into the house to get my gym bag between his passes, or just before or just after he arrived in the area. I missed him by probably two to three minutes, either coming or going. Possibly I just missed him more than once. Connie was already mowing the northeastern corner of her lawn, and this is when she saw him make his second trip around the block.

He took the same path as he did on Monday, in reverse, at least twice. Krajcir went north on Westernaire until Lakeview, where we lived, and turned left, passing my house on his right, proceeding toward the Clark and Witte houses perched on the opposite sides of the street at the intersection of Lakeview and Skyline. Then he turned left on Skyline toward Old Route 13. This pattern makes a big square, until he doubled back on Skyline toward the intersection again.

In her statement dated May 12 to the police, Connie said that she began to mow this northeastern sector of her front lawn at approximately noon. She experienced some mower trouble then. As she was trying to restart the lawnmower, she noticed the man in the silver car making his first pass by her house. When I pulled into my driveway, she was mowing full speed ahead, the issue apparently already resolved.

With my car door wide open, as well as the back door to my house, it would have been easy for someone to walk in behind me. They wouldn't even have had to leave a fingerprint. The carpeting in the house and on the stairs would have muffled any footsteps. And the kids were secured out of the way in their car seats.

At any rate, my timing on that Friday was so good at keeping out of harm's way, I feel someone was watching out for us. Maybe the powers that be were even working overtime, what with my foolishness at leaving doors wide open. Such an invitation to trouble, that I might as well have flagged Krajcir down and asked him in to tea. Even though the unsettling encounter I had with the stranger while planting flowers had occurred only that past Monday, I never, in my wildest imaginings, expected to have had any interaction with a serial killer. Especially not one who, as I was to find out many years later, was in the midst of his most deadly killing spree. Certainly, no one else in that time or place ever thought about having to deal with a serial killer, either, not even the police. But I have never again repeated my rather careless behavior when I dashed into the house to retrieve my gym bag. Even now, thirty years later, when I pull into my garage, I check to see if anyone is behind me before I close the garage door and before I unlock my car door and get out.

Chapter Six

The Aftermath

In a small town, or even in a larger place, gossip can flow like honey—and where there is honey, there are bees! Some comments could sting, and did, I'm sure. Because Virginia had been at the grocery store, theories flew in that direction on the "whodunit" meter. The manager, who was probably interviewed by the police in establishing a timeline of her movements prior to the murder, was rumored to have been questioned about the crime itself. Of course, some people always suspect the spouse, as do the police a great deal of the time.

Some people thought David Witte's timing on his return home just a few minutes after Krajcir left was too neat not to have been planned. And his statement to Connie, and repeated by him to the police, "I didn't touch anything," as if he had almost expected to find a crime scene, too prepared. He also stated he used a handkerchief to pick up a telephone at his house to make the initial call to the police. In a moment of panic and disbelief, this guy thought of everything!

And then there was his flat statement to Connie, "She's dead," too definite, too atypical for a spouse who had just stumbled onto the unthinkable.

David also had a cut on his hand which was examined by a Doctor and determined to have happened at least a week, if not more, before the crime.

It would surely be an odd police investigation that did not look at the person closest to Virginia, but the whispers continued to circulate after the police turned their attention elsewhere.

One woman from the neighborhood flatly stated to me, "I was afraid of him after that."

David Witte was not known to his immediate neighbors as a laid-back or particularly outgoing kind of guy, as opposed to Virginia, who would wave or talk to anyone. He preferred his neighbors to call him "Mr. Witte", as opposed to David, or the friendlier, Dave. He referred to Virginia as "Mrs. Witte," as well.

Lacking much personal knowledge of the man as opposed to the hard, cold facts of Virginia's murder that lovely Friday in May, it may not be entirely surprising that some people were leery of David Witte after the crime, some even going so far as suggesting a murder-for-hire scheme.

As for myself, having seen the man deemed the prime suspect and observed his behavior as he unhurriedly cruised through my neighborhood, I personally did not think "Mr. Witte" was to blame. I had received the distinct impression that this individual was looking for someone, or someplace—checking the street signs, driving slowly through the subdivision, scouting out a route, perhaps.

Or maybe, "hunting".

Not even the funeral home provided a sanctuary from rumors or the ongoing investigation. Once the body was released, after the autopsy, a visitation was held at the local funeral home for friends and family to gather one last time before services and burial.

Having donned my little black wedding/graduation/funeral dress, I came downstairs, fastening an earring as I passed the full-length window in the dining room. I stopped mid-fasten to watch as a car drove slowly past our house, toward the corner, with intent faces peering out the windows on our side of the street. The "murder house" would be coming up, and they didn't want to miss it. A family with children, for God's sake. What was there to see, I wondered? *Go away*, I thought with a flash of anger.

A good turn-out from Roger's office was already at the funeral home when we arrived. In the entry hall we signed the guest book. The first thing you saw as you stepped into the parlor was the open casket. The second, to the left, my attention diverted by a loud voice, was David Witte himself. He was gesturing broadly, telling another man that the investigation was going well and that there were plain clothes police there right now, in case the killer showed up.

The killer *here*? Did they already know who they were looking for? Did they expect him to show up? Would they pounce on him and arrest him then and there? I stopped dead in my tracks, confused. David Witte saw me and stopped talking mid-sentence, his arm drooping to his side. I was then swept through the doorway by new arrivals, toward the casket. Speaking softly with a few of Virginia's former co-workers, polite talk was murmured back-and-forth. Yes, she looks very nice, such a shame, too young to die, so tragic to die like that, who would think something like this could happen? I could feel David Witte's eyes on my back. Did he think most of the neighborhood women, including me, thought that he had played a part in his wife's murder? I would hear soft snippets of such gossip circulating that afternoon. "The husband always" — …"he did it" — "murder-for- hire".

My mind wandered to the final time I talked to Virginia. It was just a couple of days before they left on their vacation. I saw her beginning to put her plants on the front porch, as I was taking some mail across the street to my mailbox. I waved to get her attention, and asked when they were leaving. Virginia scurried across the neighbor's yard to chat briefly, her eyes twinkling with happiness. She was excited to soon see her sons and new grandbaby. Turning to go back to her house, her step was so light it was almost a skip. I tossed out a final comment; she laughed, and gave a little wave as she continued home.

I wished Virginia could somehow tell us what happened, who did this. But of course, she could not. She had passed through a doorway and that door was firmly shut to us.

Now engaged in funeral-speak beside her coffin, her eyes and step, filled with happiness, the laugh and wave lingered in my memory. And now so still.

David Witte did not remain in the area long afterwards. He took some time to get the house back in order, listing and selling it shortly thereafter, and moved back to the St. Louis area. The uneasy truce between him and his neighbors ceased. He eventually remarried but did not live long enough to see justice done. Two sons survive David and Virginia Witte.

Because this area was not densely populated, a limited pool of suspects seemed a reasonable assumption. So, some maintained the murderer was an "outsider" who maybe had just pulled off Interstate 57 bent on lunch, gas and murder. He was long gone by now, the theory continued, and the murder would never be solved.

Many people felt safer with this explanation.

One thing I had not counted on was what I began to call the" drive-bys". They began to get on my nerves, and a steady stream of strangers made me wary and uneasy. Who knew who these people were? They simply drove by the Witte house and the neighboring houses, gawking. There was nothing to see but the yellow police tape. When that came down, the stream slowed to a trickle.

Another thing I personally had not encountered before was the news media. Newspaper reporters, TV stations with vans, newscasters with microphones, everyone for miles around, briefly sent someone to cover the story. I stepped out to cross the street one time to get the mail, and noticed a woman standing in front of Connie Clark's house holding a microphone. She was speaking into it, and when she saw me, she started my way. When I saw her come towards me, I bolted back into my house.

The neighborhood had turned into a circus. Edgy though we were, we tried our best to help the police investigation.

During an interview with the police the next day after the murder, I mentioned that not THAT day, the Friday Virginia was murdered, but a few days earlier, I had seen a man who acted strangely. They asked me to describe him, and I then relayed the scene that had played itself out while I was outside planting my marigolds. Because I had gotten a pretty good look at the car, too, they seemed very interested.

This opened the floodgates. I was repeatedly asked to tell this story on several different occasions. I talked to local police, detectives, even an investigator from the State Police. Usually they came in pairs.

Per a news release from the Williamson County Sheriff's Department dated May 15, 1978, the investigation included the Marion Police Department, Williamson County Detective Unit, and the Williamson County Sheriff's Department. Not to mention the State Police Investigator I remember distinctly being interviewed by. I am sure I talked with them all, and actually I never did sort out who went with what. Having had no experience with police investigations or violent crime I did not even think of the distinctions, assuming they were all on the same team, after all. I basically told and re-told the same story again and again. They came and they went.

The first "official" statement I gave to the police was the day after the murder, May 13. A little after noon I spoke with Detective James Odom and a Sergeant Richey. I believe this was part of the random interviewing they were doing within the neighborhood. There is no indication that they came to my house specifically to talk to me. It is also the first time I began to put two-and-two together. I told them about the suspicious man I had seen that prior Monday and the vehicle he was driving. I was originally put off by the line of questioning about any unusual activities the day of the crime, and the shock and horror of the brutal crime. I was recovering my wits a bit by the next day, I think.

This, from the files, was the first time I had seen this statement. It does state that the driver was going the direction I indicated, but it does not say that he pulled up on the wrong side of the road beside me. It also does not indicate that my back was fully turned to the approaching vehicle as I kneeled on the ground, gardening. It is totally wrong in saying: "Mrs. Patterson stated that she saw the man looking at her and she smiled."

Maybe I am being picky, but I did not smile at him—I looked up to see who had stopped and I was already smiling. My smile almost immediately slipped, wondering who this rather intimidating person was and what could he possibly want. It also does not state that he actually pulled up alongside me and stopped his car completely for a couple of minutes. It does seem, reading back over this statement, that I briefly glanced up at a stranger driving slowly by, when in actuality I got a very good look at this individual from a distance of no more than 10 feet. The detectives were in a hurry to cover as much ground as possible, but I feel this statement is somewhat misleading and that they did not listen as carefully as they could have.

The statement by Captain James Odom further states that "on Monday, May 8, 1978, at about 1:00 PM, she observed an unknown man driving by her house rather slowly. Mrs. Patterson stated she was in the front lawn planting flowers when she noticed the man....with neat dark hair, in his 30's with an average build. She stated that the man was not wearing glasses. Mrs. Patterson further stated that the man was driving a silver or gray vehicle, possibly a Chevrolet or Buick. Mrs. Patterson said the vehicle was clean and shiny, 'like new'. She stated that the vehicle came from the west on Lakeview Drive going east. The driver's window was down. Mrs. Patterson stated that she saw the man looking at her and she smiled. Mrs. Patterson said that when she smiled, the man just stared at her and gave no indication of acknowledging her. Mrs. Patterson said she had not seen the man before. Reporting officer showed Mrs. Patterson a copy of the composite photos, but she said it only looked a little bit like the man she saw."

Apparently, at that time, on the Saturday after the murder, I then viewed the composite sketch Connie and the police artist went to work on almost immediately after the crime. It was shown to me in a group of about three other sketches. I was told there were "significant differences" between the drawings and to pick one. So I did. The sketch showed heavy framed glasses and I knew I had *not* seen that. It also did not include a mustache, and I knew I *had* seen that. They ran this sketch on the front page of the Marion newspaper. It was the only indication that I had that I had picked the "right one".

Again, on May 19, I again talked with Detective Odom. I had completely forgotten this episode, until finding it in the case evidence files. I think we had talked several times, and he had given me his card and told me to call him if I remembered anything else or just wanted to talk with him. I had noticed a cigarette butt under my kitchen window beside the air conditioner unit. No one in the house smoked, and we had had no workers either inside or outside of the house, (being young and relatively poor) so this did seem curiously out-of-place. And, after Virginia's murder, we had become very concerned about strangers in the neighborhood, so the cigarette butt worried me.

I watched with a faint sense of amusement as Detective Odom picked up the butt with gloved hands and tweezers, and gingerly put it into an evidence bag. I peered at the cigarette through the baggie. It was what I thought of as a "manly" cigarette—either a Camel or Marlboro, I do not remember which, and the report does not detail the brand. With all the evidence, rumored to be over a hundred items, taken from the Witte house, this was probably never looked at again. I had the feeling the detective was pacifying me, but this was part of his job, so he had to get on with it. He was not impatient. He was dealing with what he probably felt had become an all-too-familiar local hysteria by now, only one short week after the murder.

But my amusement faded, however, when I realized it had gotten there somehow, and I wearily wondered if we had, in addition to a murderer, a resident "Peeping Tom", too.

Coincidently, thirty years later, I was to find out that a woman from Cape Girardeau, Missouri, who was unfortunate enough to have Timothy Krajcir lurking in her neighborhood, had also reported cigarette butts under her back window by her air conditioner. Except this woman would not survive.

****

SPOOKED as we citizens were, we weren't the only ones. One day, two policemen showed up at my door, promptly thrusting a badge practically to my nose. They seemed a bit shaken up. Stepping back and uncrossing my eyes, I asked them if anything was wrong. They told me that they had gone to one woman's house and she met them at the door with a gun. They obviously felt this had been a close call! At any rate, they had approached my house cautiously with the badge held up high, so I could not miss it: like a shield.

I thought a gun did not sound like a bad idea. In the current atmosphere, innocence, and the feeling that we could depend on the police to protect us, was fading fast.

Of all the visits I had from the police, though, one other particularly stands out in my memory. This time a group of eight to ten investigators trooped into my front hallway and bunched up about three deep. They remained standing. The group was led by Dick Evans, an agent with the Illinois Bureau of Investigation. Trim and dapper, he appeared to be an intelligent and thoughtful man. During some initial small talk, having discovered we had only recently moved from Centralia, he mentioned a rather

51

infamous murder case there that he had once worked on. He told me that even though there had not been an arrest, he was satisfied in his own mind that he knew who was responsible. I told him, in turn, that I hoped he would be able to resolve this case *and* find and arrest the guilty party.

Once again, I began to tell my story of planting flowers and the man in the silver car, but when I mentioned that the suspect had stopped at the corner and looked up at the street signs, I paused briefly. In that quiet space of time, one of the investigators in the back of the group piped up, "He saw something he liked and came back for it."

A shocked silence gripped the room, Agent Evans half-turning toward the offending person who'd spoken, and he then cocked an eyebrow. The officer next to the outspoken officer put his hand on his shoulder and ushered him out my front door without a word. Turning back to face me once again, Evans continued smoothly on, picking up where we had left off. Momentarily speechless, I struggled to regain focus. We finished shortly afterward, and they all left together.

In hindsight, of which there is a lot of in this case, I realize that this one officer, however rudely expressed this remark might have been, had hit on a vital truth that no one else seemed to understand at the time. All the people investigating Virginia's murder, as well as those of Krajcir's other victims, considered them to be local in origin as well as fairly random, unconnected crimes. But in this "Eureka!" moment, a light bulb went off in the investigator's mind, and he realized that they weren't unconnected or necessarily local at all. That this murderer was actually a predator, someone who stalked his prey by familiarizing himself with an area and the people in it, and then came back to find and kill his victim. The fact was, a lot of women were home during the day in this area, the two roads intersecting at Skyline and Lakeview. This was where the killer had parked and looked all around before pulling into the Witte driveway. It was an area that provided good "hunting" for someone of Krajcir's bent frame of mind. Unfortunately, the officer blurted it out a little too loudly at an inopportune moment, and was escorted out for his poorly expressed insight. I have wondered since if a little more tact on his part might have made a difference in the direction of the investigation from that point on.

We decided we had had enough of the interviewing, the gawkers, the media presence and the armed camp that seemed to be springing up around us. We needed to get away for a couple of days. If memory serves me correctly, there were two separate interviews the day I started hurriedly packing. I literally packed around police of various departments. I remember holding some folded clothing items for my children in one hand, and a couple of toys to pack in the other, giving the same statement I had already given before, while standing in my front hallway.

As I was gathering up clothes and toys, the police were urging me to look closely at various models of cars with an eye to further pinning down the model of the vehicle I'd seen. They asked me to try to recall any license plate information, or stickers or decals. They also floated the idea of trying hypnosis to pull more detail from my memory. They would be in touch when I got back.

I told them I would think about it, but as he drove away, a holly bush was in the way of getting a view of the license plate. I remember seeing the taillights flash red through the holly bush when he braked and looked up at the street sign on the corner of Lakeview and Westernaire. The rest of the time the car was sideways to me.

I had indicated that I thought it was either a Chevy or possibly an Oldsmobile, definitely new and that silvery-grey color.

After we left, I did think about this quite a bit. I looked and looked until I thought I would go crazy, at any and all cars I felt were similar, while we were driving and in parking lots. I was coming around to believing it was most likely a Chevy, but felt I could not say definitely.

When we returned, I did ask some questions about hypnosis. My Dad, who worked in the Jefferson County Courthouse in Mt. Vernon, Illinois, had made his own inquiries among some of the legal professionals there. I found out that due to various court rulings this was a fuzzy area. I heard the term "unstable witness". As best as I could determine, once you had undergone hypnosis, if you were called upon to testify, this meant not that you were crazy, but that your credibility on the witness stand could be called into question. It was felt that a person under hypnosis was susceptible to being led by the interviewer to a misstatement or a wrong conclusion with sometime dire results. But besides being called "unstable"—a term which for obvious reasons anybody would prefer to avoid—I decided I would rather testify to what I knew if it came to a trial. If there was anything I could do to help convict this person, I wanted to give it without taint.

In the end, I decided I probably could not offer any more information, and I declined the hypnosis.

One further incident, after we returned home, again resulted in more jangled nerves. And, because I felt that the cooperation I had already extended to the police had done little good and instead had totally disrupted, in particular, my children's lives, as well as my own, I did not report this to the police.

Since we were new in the community, having only moved in five months ago and had not had time, as yet, to make any enemies, we thought this was only a random occurrence. Maybe, maybe not. Shortly after the talk and the cigarette-butt evidence-gathering with Detective Odom, seven days after the murder, at midnight I was awakened by a ringing telephone. It was one of those middle-of-the-night occurrences where you come instantly awake. I picked up the telephone which was on my side of the bed and mumbled, "Hello".

A man's voice, fairly young and very crisp, and official-sounding, (I thought he was actually a police officer) asked to speak to my husband. As my husband's parents were currently traveling, I thought perhaps something had happened to them. I asked who was calling and he replied, "William Shoemaker." I did not know who this person was, but immediately handed over the phone to Roger, saying, "It's for you." I leaned in close to hear what the caller had to say.

After Roger said "Hello," the caller dropped his brisk phone voice and started screaming obscenities in a loud and angry voice into his ear. Roger, in astonishment, held the phone out, and we could both clearly hear him ranting. He quickly finished up with "I want to SEE your wife. I'm going to SEE your wife!"

I snatched the telephone away, leapt out of bed and hung it up, standing over the nightstand, staring down at it and holding my hand as if it had been bitten by a live thing.

I don't recall much discussion on the matter, but Roger immediately went downstairs to the basement, returning with a loaded hunting rifle. Both chilled now, we climbed back into bed, with the rifle tucked underneath his side of the bed. We slept that way for several nights thereafter. The world had simply gone mad, and literally anything could happen.

I did not call the Detective again because I did not think this obscene phone call was something they could do much about. After all, they did not seem to have made much headway on a murder case. I might have changed my mind if I had been aware that another woman, also on Lakeview, had a similar experience.

Per an Investigative Report dated 5/14/78, two days after the murder, one woman had received "a harassing telephone call." Apparently the phone rang about 9 p.m.

The report continues, "When she answered the phone, a male voice asked if she would like some company and if he could come over and see her. The caller, giving both a first and last name, said his name was "Bob Thomas....caller further stated something concerning a 'Head Job' ".

She hung up the telephone at that point, and the police duly noted this. It is included in the Witte case files, so they must have felt at the time that the murderer could have had some involvement. The fact that he used a complete, made-up name, as did my caller, within a week or so after the murder, does not seem coincidental.

****

AFTER our brief trip to Paducah, Kentucky, we returned to a quieter neighborhood. The media had decamped. The detectives were still coming around, but not so often. Fewer gawkers were around, the police tape having been removed from the Witte house. We could breathe a small sigh of relief, at last, even though a simmering tension still hummed throughout the neighborhood.

People dealt with the immediate period after this murder as best they could. The Clarks also left town for a few days. Some neighbors, who did stay, on Lakeview Drive and just west of the intersection of Skyline and Lakeview, hired a private security service to monitor their lives and property. They stayed for about a week after the murder, according to the recollections of Sherry Austin, one of the neighbors who had hired the guard service.

55

Also, we did not know then that Krajcir, the killer, worked mainly at night. It would have been easy for him to walk the railroad tracks behind the houses on Lakeview, partially hidden due to the lower elevation of the tracks and brush. We all assumed that the houses on the northern side of Lakeview Drive had privacy, and we did not always bother to pull curtains or drapes in the back windows of our houses, if we even had them. In our upstairs bathroom window, for instance, we only had some sheer Priscilla curtains. The land behind was undeveloped with no street. It was "Peeping Tom" heaven: dark, quiet, and secluded.

So, maybe it was a good thing there was some sort of patrol presence on the street at that time, particularly at night.

And no wonder people were spooked. After all, Virginia had been killed in the short span of time between pulling into her driveway and her husband's arrival home, all within about an hour. Some felt that Virginia's movements had to have been known by the killer that day, an atypical and busy day for her. Even if this was someone who knew her or her husband, or was even a murder-for-hire, the fact was that there was still a cold-blooded killer out there. It seemed one could not be too careful.

One of the interviewing policemen cautioned me to stay alert, because the suspect might come back to "the scene of the crime", so to speak.

I remember this warning clearly, even though at the time it seemed to be a chance remark made off-handedly—and I admit I was already a bit unnerved about a potential re-visit from this man I knew had been in and out of our neighborhood twice. A local psychologist, whose office was located on the town square, and who I presume had some contact with the local police, also located on the town square, had called me with the advice to be very careful, leaving me with the chilling admonishment that this was an individual with brutal, homicidal tendencies, possibly a psychopath with a violent temper.

But, still no one viewed this as more than an isolated incident. Awareness of linkage to other, similar unsolved crimes, with modern databases and DNA usage in forensic science was not in the realm of possibility then. I had tried to comfort myself with the thought that this person was looking through the neighborhood for an easy entry for what I thought was a planned crime of rape or robbery. Something must have gone horribly wrong. Perhaps Virginia had taken the knife out of the kitchen drawer herself, to ward off her attacker, and a struggle had ensued. But it turns out he was already an accomplished burglar and did not view a locked door or window as a deterrent. And she never got much of a chance to try to defend herself at all. I realized he was dangerous, but I had no idea to what extent.

I thought it was time that I asked to borrow my dad's handgun. It was great weather for the kids to play outside and I was unwilling to stay huddled behind locked doors. I knew how to load the bullets. I had even done some target practice with this handgun before, a .22 nickel-plated revolver. It seemed heavy, and I needed both hands to hold and steady it to even take aim. My mom drove the pistol and ammunition the approximately 44 miles to me.

Was I capable of pulling the trigger? Yes, I think so, at least in self-defense. Was I able to hit what I intended? Probably the next-door neighbor's garage would have taken a mortal wound, but the gun itself might render taking a shot unnecessary.

I hoped.

The kids had a swing set and a sandbox in the backyard. I was not much in favor of spending time in the front yard just then. Besides, the sandbox had a small shade tree beside it with a notch, beyond the children's reach, perfect for stashing the handgun.

About three weeks after Virginia's funeral, just when things were returning to normal, a terrible thunderstorm began to gather a little after noon. The kids had had their lunch. I took them upstairs for their naps and I returned to the kitchen to wash up the dishes. I had a big window over the sink which overlooked the back yard and the little railroad tracks and what was then the empty field beyond. I glanced out anxiously, wondering if I should be on the lookout for a possible tornado.

My eyes wandered to the northwest, where a burst of brilliant sunlight was slowly being squeezed shut by the lowering cloud bank. And there, perfectly illuminated by that shaft of bright light, sat a man in a silver car. He was parked beyond the tracks just north of the Witte house, on Skyline Drive. He was looking in his rear view mirror back at the Witte house. His build and the car were too familiar.

My heart stopped suddenly with a painful thud in my chest. I couldn't breathe.

The storm clouds began to thicken and lower, hanging dark and heavy. They wrapped around the car, beginning to dim my view. Little by little, the man became a silhouette and the color of the car began to fade into the darker tint of the lowering clouds.

I ran to my phone. In the drawer under the telephone was a card one of the detectives had given me. (Perhaps the evidence-gathering Detective Odom.) I dialed, asking for him. I was told he was not available. I identified myself and told the person on the other end that a man and a car matching the description of the murderer were currently parked just north of the Witte house. I asked that they send someone out as soon as possible.

The dispatcher sounded a little weary, but said someone would be out soon. Breathlessly, I begged her again to *please* send someone immediately.

I returned to the window and gripped the edge of the kitchen sink. Still there. Still looking back at the house. Please, hurry, hurry, I begged silently over and over.

Out of nowhere, I suddenly had a wild impulse to run through the backyard and up to the driver's door. He was gloating, smiling, reliving his deeds, I was sure. I wanted to beat on the car door, yank open the door and pummel the man. I wanted to say, "What are you doing? Why did you do this?"

All the while this somehow satisfying little scenario was playing in my mind, I was aware of my sleeping little ones upstairs. It felt as though a physical weight was on my shoulders, holding me in place. I could not leave, I could not run through the backyard, I could not pummel. I could only watch helplessly, my heart hammering in my chest.

I was pacing frantically back and forth between the telephone, willing it to ring, to say help was on the way, to the window, willing a police car to show up and detain the man. Back and forth, like a caged animal.

Hurry, hurry, repeatedly sounded inside my head like a mantra.

The storm cloud was now so low and black it had almost obliterated the vehicle itself. It seemed to have wrapped around the car like a shroud, little, blowing finger-like tendrils of dark cloud and heavy mist pointing down toward the ground. I remained standing there, clutching the edge of the sink, staring out the window, still chanting to myself, hurry, hurry. Please hurry.

Then, just seconds before the rain broke in a heavy deluge the man ever so slowly eased his car away towards Highway New 13. I waited in vain for any response from the police that day.

It would be many, many years before I would see this man again or learn who he was. But at the time, even though I recognized this person and was fairly sure he had assaulted and murdered my neighbor, I did not think to go get my father's gun. I phoned for help. And prayed it would come.

I wonder, thirty years later, if all, or even a few, of Timothy Krajcir's victims-yet-to-be or their families would applaud how I handled the situation.

I heard nothing further from the police. Asking for my statements to the police, I found that only a few are currently in the case file. One, typed on green paper and dated that December, makes note of a call I placed to police inquiring about the investigation at that time. I, like so many others, did occasionally ask about progress on this case. Possibly the quiet surrounding the Witte house that approaching Christmas prompted a hopeful call for any news on the case. At any rate, I then inquired what had happened to the dispatch of an officer to investigate my call concerning the man parked beyond the Witte house.

After a heavy pause, I was told there is no record of this call to the Marion police department.

So, at the very first, this little enclave called Westernaire Estates, perched on the then-outer-most western edge of the town of Marion, Illinois, had seemed like an ideal little neighborhood. Adults as well as young families with small children would simply do normal, everyday things on bicycles and in backyards. A sense of community presided over this small, middle-American town where doors might or might not be locked, and where we could feel safe and secure in our little routines and in our homes.

Once this tranquility was broken, we felt, eventually, somewhat safe once again.

Like a patient recovering from a breakdown, we needed some time to steady our collective nerves.

But something had been lost and was not recovered. Doors were locked; strangers not so welcome, and never let into houses. I myself never pulled into my driveway again without looking over my shoulder to see if anyone had pulled in behind me or had followed me home. And, once inside, my doors were locked.

We got on with our lives as best we could, and the one, best chance for stopping this serial killer was lost, leaving Krajcir to also go on with his life, but taking others along the way.

PART TWO

CRACKING A COLD CASE

Chapter Seven

A Break in the Case

The investigative effort to solve the murder of my neighbor, Virginia Witte, began unraveling with a DNA match of evidence in the Sheppard case, which pointed to Timothy Krajcir. Lieutenant Paul Echols was determined to pursue all avenues to solve this haunting case: the April 8, 1982 murder of a beautiful, black co-ed, raped, beaten about the head, and strangled in her Carbondale apartment the month before her graduation from Southern Illinois University.

Her body had been found face down on her bed; when they turned her over, some liquid trickled from her mouth onto her shirt. The shirt, after some discussion as to its relevance to the crime scene, was duly, and luckily, preserved as evidence even though no technology at the time could identify to whom this liquid might belong.

In August, 2007, the cracking of this cold case was big news in southern Illinois and southeastern Missouri. The coverage had not reached the St. Louis media, as yet, but it was widely covered just a bit farther south.

And so, about 50 miles away, across the mighty Mississippi River in Cape Girardeau, Missouri, Detective Jimmy Smith was watching with intense interest as Lieutenant Paul Echol's case unfolded. He had a gut feeling that somehow, a few cold cases of his own might also be the work of Krajcir. He pulled together in his mind the varied pieces of unsolved crimes and saw there were some similarities.

The time frame seemed to fit, Krajcir not having been in prison at the time of Smith's unsolved crimes, and he was in the vicinity. Other things seemed similar, too; the laces he bound some of his victims with, the types of knots used, the blue bandana he sometimes tied over the lower half of his face during the sexual assaults, and the position the bodies of the murder victims were found in—too many little coincidences scattered throughout different cases.

In August 2007, Detective Jimmy Smith called Lieutenant Echols to compare notes on his unsolved crimes.

Lieutenant Echols did not feel there was any reason to assume Krajcir was in Cape Girardeau, Missouri, at those times.

But, after Echols dug further into Krajcir's background, this tireless, highly organized investigator discovered that while employed by an ambulance crew in Carbondale, Krajcir would almost certainly have worked transporting patients in and around the area. And Cape Girardeau was very likely one town he would have visited.

Lieutenant Echols and Detective Jimmy Smith began to seriously compare notes. They were nearly certain they could use DNA evidence from sexual assaults against Krajcir, but murder?

They were sure he had murdered Deborah Sheppard. But what about the other unsolved murders in Missouri? Were there more victims out there?

And here two legendary, modern-day lawmen begin to unravel the twisted life and crimes of Timothy Krajcir. Luck, tenacity, experience and investigative instinct came to the fore, and brought together these men who were able to reach back, as far ago as thirty years, to bring a violent criminal and murderer to justice.

Lieutenant Paul Echols, with his blue eyes, light blondish-brown hair of the Carbondale, Illinois police department, and Detective Jimmy Smith, with predominantly gray salt-and-pepper hair and dark, almond-shaped eyes, of the Cape Girardeau, Missouri police became a team by osmosis, seemingly, so closely and diligently did they begin to work together. A part of this legend will include the chance photo of a DNA sequence, taken in a moment of high spirits. A little earlier, in August 2007, Lieutenant Echols had awaited DNA results at the Illinois State Crime Lab. A hit registered on the Illinois prison population's database. A key to unlock the murder of Deborah Sheppard was then in Echol's hands.

He was elated, and took a picture with his cell phone of the DNA data that would point to Timothy Krajcir as the murderer of Deborah Sheppard.

As the two began to determine the best way to discover any links between Krajcir and the unsolved murder cases, Lieutenant Echols remembered his DNA photo at a critical moment to their investigations.

It seems the Missouri Crime Lab was not willing to run a further test on the DNA evidence collected at homicide victim Mildred Wallace's home, having done a prior test a few years earlier, without results. Detective Jimmy Smith could not get them to budge.

But armed with his photo, Echols located a DNA technician and asked him to do a comparison for him, rather than asking for a new test.

They got confirmation that Timothy Krajcir, indeed, was connected to the 1982 murder of Mildred Wallace in Cape Girardeau.

Finally, after all these years, we had some valid leads and things were beginning to come together.

They had gone to question Krajcir at Big Muddy Correctional Center on November 14, 2007 and he then denied his connection to any unsolved crimes in Cape Girardeau. Serving the remainder of a child molestation sentence after violating his parole since 1983, he had nothing to gain by confessing to murders that could put him on death row.

But after Krajcir was allowed to view laboratory reports from the Wallace case on DNA comparisons (unfortunately only 1 in 780,000), and that of a palm print found on Mrs. Wallace's window (a definite match), they began to talk. Smith steered the conversation to Krajcir's cooperation in other investigations if the death penalty could be waived. "I don't think you could do that", was Krajcir's response. Smith assured him he would try. Krajcir allowed that he would listen if that were to happen.

It was ultimately the decision of Cape Girardeau County Prosecuting Attorney, Morley Swingle. Smith reached him at his home that evening with his thoughts on the waiver. He did not immediately agree, but between November 14, 2007, and November 26, 2007 further discussions took place. Swingle also talked with the victim's families. Ultimately, the family members felt that a confession would bring closure to others, as well as themselves. It had to be unanimous. It was.

After the flurry of activity between Krajcir and Smith and Echols and legal processes in four states, as well as the families, Krajcir finally received, on November 26, 2007, via his attorney, a letter from Swingle detailing how the waiver of the death penalty in Mrs. Wallace's murder would work. He needed to make full confession to his crimes, and any significant lie would mean he would be tried on capital murder charges.

Subsequently, he then, on December 3, 2007, confessed to murders, robberies and sexual assaults that they had no actual physical evidence to link him to. He confessed to murdering in Pennsylvania Myrtle Rupp, age 51, in 1979, while Krajcir was in that area visiting family; in Kentucky, Joyce Tharp, age 29, kidnapped, assaulted and murdered at Krajcir's home in Carbondale, Illinois, and her nude body returned to Kentucky to be dumped behind a church, in 1979; and Illinois as well as Missouri. He also admitted to over 50 sexual assaults, stealing and breaking-and-entering.

The detectives were to try to get as many detailed confessions out of Krajcir before the December 10, 2007 court date where Krajcir was expected to plead guilty to the Deborah Sheppard murder. At any time, they felt, he could stop talking to them. They feared after his removal from Big Muddy, where he was reasonably comfortable, he could stop being cooperative. His transfer to a state supermax prison probably would not be to Krajcir's liking, with all his little freedoms gone. No more prison ball games were in his future.

In the aftermath of his confessions, the relief to the victims' families and friends was evident. Echols and Smith were heroes to many people, given awards, citations and even invited to reunions of victims' families.

At a meeting with the families in Cape Girardeau both Echols and Smith were given a standing ovation. Smith handed

66

out white roses to surviving family members. It was a heartfelt gesture; both detectives had gotten to know these people and felt genuine sympathy for them. They had shared in the pain and frustration felt by everyone present that day.

Detective Jimmy Smith says he "think(s) of them (the victims) each and every day. I have told them all, 'I feel that God had always heard the many prayers over the years from all the family and others, and finally decided that it was time to answer those prayers, and doing so, he used me as his helper.' " He further says that he "has to feel that way knowing what I know about each of the cases and the families involved."

And, for the families and friends, Lieutenant Paul Echols and Detective Jimmy Smith represent the human face of law enforcement and justice. The survivors must have felt that the system had been cold, unresponsive and uncaring at times, but here stood two men saying their loved ones had not been forgotten, and the wheels of justice had not, in fact, stopped turning in their behalf. They had not given up, and indeed, had solved these horrible crimes, bringing closure at long last.

In Missouri, Krajcir was charged with five murders. The Cape Girardeau County Prosecuting Attorney, Morey Swingle, had been ready to proceed all the way to the death penalty.

If anyone ever deserved the death penalty, then Timothy Krajcir most certainly does.

I spoke with John Volkerding, Investigator with the Prosecuting Attorney's office in Cape Girardeau County. He stated that Mr. Swingle "was not initially in favor of waiving the death penalty".

The Prosecuting Attorney's decision, Mr. Volkerding stressed, subsequently obtained the "confessions to the Witte murder and the Tharp abduction and murder, of which no DNA evidence was obtained."

On November 14, 2007, Smith and Echols, at Big Muddy Correctional Center gave the prisoner a lot to think about, mentioning waiving the death penalty. Up to that time, he had denied any knowledge of any of the unsolved crimes.

After the December guilty plea, prosecutor Swingle immediately prepared a warrant for five murders and rape. Krajcir's confessions allowed them to prepare a Probable Cause statement for new charges. This set out the reasons why they believed Krajcir was guilty of these additional crimes of home invasion, robbery, and assault.

Krajcir's activities expanded beyond Carbondale, Illinois when he headed west into the Cape Girardeau, Missouri area. This is about a 45 minute drive from where he lived in a trailer on the edge of Carbondale. The assumption has been made that he familiarized himself with this area via ambulance runs with patients while on his job.

He returned on his own, to "hunt." A creature of the night, he liked areas under the cover of darkness, where he could more easily follow his targeted victims home and even look into their windows. He particularly liked women who lived alone.

Between 1977 and 1982 alone, he committed, or so far has admitted, to five murders, seven sexual assaults and a robbery of an elderly couple in their home.

A brief overview of the 1979-1988 timeframe might be helpful at this time:

In 1979 Krajcir was imprisoned under the Sexually Dangerous Person statute after he was found guilty of raping a 13-year-old in Carbondale, Illinois. Some accounts say she was the daughter of his landlord, some say of a friend. The actual molestation began in 1977, when the child was eleven, and was at the time of his arrest progressing to her younger sister. One of the parents found out, and called the police.

The police found a gun in his trailer. It was the same caliber as that used in the murders of Mary Parsh, 58, and Brenda Parsh, 27, mother and daughter, and college student Shelia Cole, who was only three years out of high school. These women were all murdered in 1977, in Cape Girardeau.

The girls' testimony led to his conviction as a sexual predator, which was then a newly-coined term that supposedly would put him away, under psychiatric care, for an indefinite period. If he appeared unstable and a threat to society, then he would remain behind bars.

He was sent to Menard State Prison for two years where he stayed until 1981.

But by 1982 he was conditionally released, more or less "cured". He continued psychiatric treatment as one of the conditions of his parole. He resumed his life in Carbondale.

Armed with the EMT license he earned while in prison, he was able to obtain employment. He also enrolled in what we now would call the Criminal Justice Program (there's irony for you) at Southern Illinois University at Carbondale. He took psychology courses to "try to figure (himself) out." He told Detectives he "did a piss poor job" of that. One of the students attending the university at that time was one Paul Echols, although they may not have attended any actual classes together.

Six months after he murdered Mildred Wallace in Cape Girardeau in June, 1982, Krajcir moved back to Pennsylvania, close to family in Allentown, Pennsylvania. He did not inform his parole officer, however. He immediately got busy preying on women through early 1983. While there, he robbed two women, stole from them, made them undress and fondled at least one of them. This particular crime spree ended when he was picked up lurking on a parking lot by police who simply wondered what he was doing there.

He was found with a loaded gun. As a convicted felon, this was a parole violation, enough to put him in jail. He was less than a model prisoner, however. He tried to escape with another inmate and ended up, via a tying-the-bed-sheets method of escape, falling and breaking his leg. His troubles were compounded when he was convicted for crimes in Pennsylvania. He was put away for these for five years, and was then transferred to Illinois, to Big Muddy, in 1988. He had violated the conditions of his parole in Illinois and would therefore be held on the basis of being a sexual predator, the therapy sessions once again offered to him.

Big Muddy Correctional Center in Ina, Illinois, is a few miles south of the larger town of Mt. Vernon. It perches on the east side of Interstate 57, and is directly across the highway from a community college. Incarcerated there are a high number of sexual offenders, said Lieutenant Schueler, of Internal Affairs. The facility provides, according to him, rehabilitation for this type of offender.

And, actually, Krajcir could once more have submitted to the sexual offender counseling program. He was smart enough to fly under the radar, so to speak, while taking advantage of job training and the counseling program. He was generally an enthusiastic participant in the group sessions, and knew what was expected of him. He probably could once again have been deemed "cured" and released. He had done it before, and he could have done it again. But Krajcir did not partake of any of the programs, thereby staying in the correctional facility. Lieutenant Echols says he feels he did not want out, and he feels this is to Krajcir's credit. He knew if he got out, he would offend again, hurting more women in the process. Apparently the counseling and rehabilitation program was not something that Krajcir, himself, knew would help him but an awareness of the fact that he *would* re-offend seems to have been a deterrent and motivation to stay in prison. And, he more or less liked his life at the facility. He played sports, held a prison job and was freed from acting out his compulsions.

So there he remained until Detectives Jim Smith of Cape Girardeau and Lieutenant Paul Echols of the Carbondale police departments showed up to interview him about some of their cold cases.

After the crack in the cold cases tied to Krajcir, as well as the accident that delivered a crack to the back of my head (just a little pun there), I was eager not only for some answers to long-held questions, but wanted to also express my appreciation to the people who had finally gotten justice for so many. Since I had started talking to Detective Christina Morrow in Marion, Illinois, and then talked with and emailed Lieutenant Echols of the Carbondale, Illinois, police, I decided to go and see them. We were all in a celebratory frame of mind.

I was fortunate to secure some time with them on back-to-back days. Connie and I had talked in the meantime. She maintained an apartment in Marion, which she offered to me. I planned on staying a day or two with her and for us both to talk with the Detective and Lieutenant.

Unfortunately, as a "military mom," Connie was called to duty. A brand-new grandson was in need of loving care while his Army mom was sent to training and his Army Special Forces dad was actively preparing to leave for Afghanistan.

So she lent me her lovely apartment, and I kept her updated. I decided to use a recorder so she could listen to the conversation later if she wished, at a more convenient time, and also because I have a hearing loss. I wanted to "get it right" after waiting almost thirty years for answers.

Both Detective Tina Morrow, who said she "would clear her calendar," and Lieutenant Echols were generous with their time. Naively I was thinking as I went to talk with them that my questions would have pat answers, and that those answers would not raise more questions.

It was only after the meetings with Detective Morrow and Lieutenant Echols that I began to write down what I was learning, and also I realized some answers would have to come from the case file itself. Those voices from the past that had once been at the epicenter of the investigation were now, for the most part, accessible only through their written words from years ago, but could yet be heard. And, as I told Lieutenant Echols, "This is a case of the tail (tale) wagging the dog."

I think he knows exactly what I mean.

Chapter Eight

Detective Christina Morrow, Marion, Illinois Police Department

January 29, 2008

Detective Morrow opened the interview by stating that having met with Krajcir, "He seems like an everyday kind of person, but you have to keep in mind he is capable of much darker things. (He has) a deeper and darker side that may have been more active when he was younger. Just because he's older, he's a frail and aging little old man now, that doesn't go away. You have to keep that in mind when dealing with this."

After being "caught" by Lieutenant Paul Echols, Carbondale police, in the Deborah Sheppard case, he now had murder charges against him. Originally he denied having anything to do with this case, but being presented with the DNA evidence he decided to bargain his way to a confession.

When Virginia Witte was murdered in Illinois in 1978, there was no death penalty in the state. This is a fact that no interviewing police have bothered to point out to Krajcir, and they are not aware if he knows it or not. He has been held as a sexually deviant person in the prison system thus far. However, his subsequent confessions to murder in Pennsylvania and in Missouri and the abduction and subsequent death in Illinois of a Kentucky woman have made him subject to the death penalty.

This punishment Krajcir apparently wishes to avoid at all costs.

Detective Morrow thinks Krajcir had "been waiting any day for somebody to come knocking on the door" to ask him to confess. He also said during his interview with her that, "Maybe I'll start writing some of these things down now so I don't have to carry them all around with me."

I wondered why, if he had been waiting to unburden himself, he didn't say something sooner. After all, I pointed out, he's been in custody most of his life and was surrounded by nothing but authority figures available to confess to.

Detective Morrow's response was that he could not confess before, because nobody knew of hard evidence that pointed to him. She feels that as a convicted rapist, he knew he would remain in prison based on that, and there was no motivation for telling. (Also, there was that pesky death penalty he preferred to avoid.)

I asked her if he might want notoriety.

Detective Morrow feels that, "At this point in time, I don't think it's about notoriety. I don't think he wants the publicity of a serial killer."

He said, "The media is making me out to be a monster."

And, the detective told me, "Here's where I had to hold my tongue, because my first initial thought is, 'You are', but having to deal with him on a face-to-face basis, I couldn't shut that door to where he wouldn't want to talk to me."

To keep him talking, she said to him, "Well, the media always makes things worse than they appear."

Then he apparently "spoke about things inside the house that basically he had to have been inside that house".

I prompted, "Such as—?"

"Well, the discovery in the webbing of her left hand, there was a cut. And she had a towel in her hand. And that was how she was found inside that residence. None of that stuff was ever put in the paper."

"He said he had one of the kitchen knives and she had actually grabbed the knife at one point. She had grabbed the blade side and he said, 'I let it go'."

Detective Morrow, probably somewhat incredulously, asked him, "You actually relinquished the knife to her?"

Krajcir: "Yeah."

Detective Morrow: "Why?"

Krajcir: "I didn't want her to cut herself."

However, before she could turn the knife on him, he snatched it back, cutting her hand. Nobody else knew that but the killer and the police.

This occurred in the hall bathroom beside the front bedroom. Virginia's body was found on the bed in the Master bedroom with a bloody towel she had apparently used to wrap her injured hand in.

Other details he divulged concerned the dog the Wittes owned. It had been a boxer, and the type of dog was never told to the media. When he stepped in through the back door, the dog ran to meet him, and he just let the dog continue on out the door. The dog did not come back to bark or scratch at the door.

I told Detective Morrow, "Actually, the dog went across the street to Connie's house. He was barking at her. She told me just the other day over the telephone, 'If I'd just gone across the street'."

I told her I had said to Connie, "then you would have knocked at the door, and you would have been in that house, too. And you would have been a victim."

Detective Morrow: "Absolutely."

Then Detective Morrow said something that surprised me: "He admits openly this was the only daytime murder he committed. Everything else was pre-planned, at nighttime, under the cover of darkness. He says he doesn't know why, specifically, he thought it was an opportunity. He was driving around by the shopping center, saw her come out, and followed her home."

Me: "That's what he says."

Detective Morrow: "That's what he says."

Detective Morrow continued, "He had a box in the car, and he pretended to deliver it to the door. He knocked on the door, Virginia opened the door and he stepped into the house. He said he had a package delivery for her and that's when he saw the dog. I asked him if the dog barked, if the dog acted aggressively, he said, 'No, not really. When I stepped in, the dog ran out the door. The dog never did come back; I don't know where it went'."

Krajcir then stated, "I was pretty frantic. It was the only daytime I ever done."

He estimated he was in the house for only 15 or 20 minutes.

Me: "There weren't a lot of signs of struggle, were there? Throughout the house?"

Morrow: "No, not a lot torn up. They initially thought this was a robbery, because the purse was knocked upside down on the floor of the kitchen. He said either one of them could have knocked the purse off the counter."

They started out in the kitchen, through the great room, then back toward the bedrooms and bathrooms. A sexual assault took place in the front bedroom, just to the right of the hallway leading back toward the other bedrooms. They proceeded to the hall bathroom, where he forced Virginia to at least partially disrobe and climb onto the stool.

According to Krajcir, he had a knife with him (he owned a buck knife) and he had taken a knife from the kitchen.

I asked why they went to the hall bathroom rather than straight to the Master bedroom.

Morrow's reply was, "Well, he's a sexually deviant person, so he was going to drag out some of the sexual escapades of his twisted mind. In the bathroom was where she grabbed the knife. The medicine cabinet was open and a box of band-aids was in the trash can and a band-aid wrapper was on the basin of the sink. And she had asked to get a band-aid.

"His mentality was he was going to have her step up on the toilet and disrobe at knife-point before he sexually assaulted her. This is where she grabbed the knife. So, she was scrapping, whether or not it was to come to a positive end, but she was scrapping. She was trying to defend herself even though there weren't lots of indications in the house of an overt struggle."

I asked if she was trying to talk to him, to reason with him. Detective Morrow said she had asked Krajcir if she was frantic or was she trying to talk to him.

Krajcir answered, "No, she seemed very calm."

Virginia's body was found on the bed in the master bedroom. Krajcir claims not to have known this was, in fact, the master bedroom, but as to size, location, the decoration, attached bath, that seems not very credible. A bloody towel and a bloody shirt were found on the bed along with her bra, and the rest of her clothing, folded, was probably originally on the bed, but was knocked to the floor.

Cause of death as ruled by the coroner was strangulation. Krajcir indicated that when he was done with the sexual assault, he strangled her. He said he did this for at least four minutes, but was not sure she was dead.

Apparently her body was convulsing and he wanted to be very sure she was dead.

So, he used the knife he took from the kitchen and tried to slash or stab her with it, leaving numerous puncture wounds. It was too dull to adequately penetrate the skin. Discarding this knife onto the bedroom chair, he went back to the kitchen to get another knife. He then slashed open her upper abdominal area and then buried the knife under her left breast.

The Coroner indicated Virginia was probably deceased or was dying at the time of the stabbing, as her heart had slowed its beating. Lack of a broad splatter pattern of blood from lack of pumping action by the heart probably kept the blood flow from the wounds to a relative minimum, pooling underneath the body.

I saw the layout of the house he had drawn for them that was very good. Detective Morrow had never been in the house. I told her that this was a very good rendering of the floor plan. After all this time, I could not have done better. And I was in and out of that house on several occasions, not just for about half an hour.

The car was a 1979 Chevy Nova. It was described by me and Connie and several other neighbors out and about that day. Detective Morrow mentioned the car dealership had contacted Krajcir.

He said, "I guess they never got around to knocking on my door."

Every car dealership in the tri-State area, including rental agencies were contacted, she indicated.

Me: "They never talked to him?"

Detective Morrow attributes this to lack of manpower for follow-up.

I protested, "He's just down the road, you know?"

Detective Morrow: "Absolutely. And when I look back, oh

my gosh, his name is here (on the dealer's list submitted to the police)."

I mentioned that in a prior telephone conversation with Lieutenant Echols of Carbondale police, Echols mentioned a partial palm print had been found on a table in the great room. I asked if it matched Krajcir's.

"They were never able to match that palm print with anybody's. I don't believe they will now, with the confession."

Me: "What made him decide to kill some women and not others? He has a lot of sexual crimes to his credit, right? Why did he kill Virginia?"

Detective Morrow: "I don't have—I don't know why. The thing he told Lieutenant Echols (during their interview) was, 'I'm not like you. I don't think about things the same way you do. I have compulsions and I have urges, and I'm not like you'."

Me: "Did he ever have any psych evaluations? Does he have any mental illness diagnosis at all?"

Detective Morrow explained he had had one when he was a young adult, based on a sexual assault and attempted murder in the Chicago area. He felt he could do nothing right, had a dominant, hard-to please mother who was not always there for him.

Krajcir was in the Navy at Great Lakes Naval Training Center when he sexually assaulted a woman who tried to leave him, possibly to check on a child. He thought she was trying to get away and he stabbed her.

He was in and out of jail from that time on and was classified as a sexually dangerous person.

Detective Morrow continued, "He confessed to three assaults of three elderly women in the Marion area."

I told her I vaguely remembered some of this.

"Weren't a couple of these women assaulted in front of their husbands?" I asked.

Detective Morrow confirmed they were. She said based on her own observations, that if a man was present the women did not die.

This might have been an interesting scenario if Virginia's husband had arrived home a little earlier from his luncheon. Would she have lived? Would Krajcir have attempted to flee, or would he have attacked David Witte, too?

Me: "Was the assault itself, when the husbands were present, was it more straightforward sex? "

"It was more deviant."

Me: "MORE deviant?"

Detective Morrow: "Well, a sexual assault is of itself a deviant act, but some of these things were kind of twisted. There was an elderly lady who was afraid for the health of her husband. So, the husband was tied up. She was tied up. He wanted the wife to lie across her husband's lap while he sexually assaulted her, on the floor, in the hallway of the living room."

"And she told Krajcir her husband had a 'heart problem, I can't do that.' "

"So he did masturbatory things in front of the woman while her husband watched. He ejaculated on her."

He also stole from them. It is believed he followed at least one of these women home from church. He was back to his cover of darkness, from which he never deviated again after the Witte murder. He also may have been in the house already when one or more of these women came home. He stole handguns which he used on other victims.

Me: "He didn't always do the same things, did he?"

Detective Morrow: "He mixed it up. His mind is dark and cobwebbed and creative, and that's what he did. Whatever he could come up with. But the women who suffered and gave up their lives, they were alone."

Me: "What about women who had people present, such as children? I understand he raped a woman who had a child present."

Detective Morrow: "Yes. And that was one of the women up in Chicago. She had a small child and he took her into another room, started to sexually assault her there. The child started to cry out. She got up to tend to her child. So, he stabbed her with a pair of scissors, and then he fled."

She was badly wounded, but survived.

"In Cape Girardeau, we have a mother and daughter, both adults. They were killed, both of them. (One of) The sad part(s) about that is he actually missed killing the mother the first time. Sexually assaulted them, tied them up on the bed, shot

Series of old kill

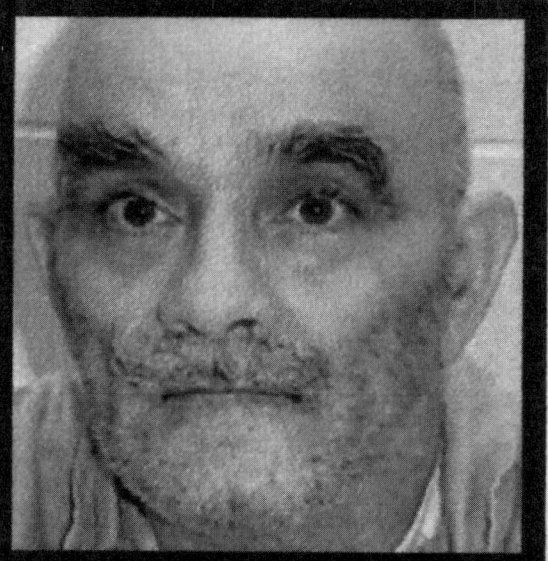

<< **TIMOTHY KRAJCI**
student Sheila Cole of

By Christine Byers, Greg Jonsson
and Heather Ratcliffe
ST. LOUIS POST-DISPATCH

CAPE GIRARDEAU, MO. • Sheila
Cole's parents went to their graves
wondering who killed their daughter.

From 1977, when he got the
news his daughter had been abducted and murdered until his
own death in 1987, Harold L. Cole
was haunted by questions.

"He would say there's not a
minute of the day or night that he

'IT'S SAD HE EVER GOT OUT' • Qu

HABITUAL SEXUAL OFFENDER ADM

MARY PARSH

BRENDA PARSH

SHEILA COLE

MARG

ings solved

confesses to slayings, including that of SEMO restwood in 1977, in return for life term.

didn't wonder what happened," said family friend Janet Hilderbrand of Kirkwood.

It was a frustration shared by Henry Gerecke, chief of police in Cape Girardeau from 1974 to 1981, as he tried to solve a string of brutal murders including that of Sheila Cole, a student from Crestwood who attended Southeast Missouri State University.

"I remember ... her father called me and said her mother was dying of cancer and asked 'Can't you tell me something?'" Gerecke

said. "And I couldn't tell them anything."

Finally, on Monday, answers came in the decades-old crimes — too late for Sheila Cole's parents, but to the relief of surviving friends and family of several women authorities say were victims of accused serial killer Timothy Wayne Krajcir.

Already behind bars in Illinois as a habitual sexual offender, Krajcir was charged Monday in the

PLEASE SEE **MURDERS** | A5

tions remain as to why Krajcir was repeatedly freed from prison. A5

TS SIX BISTATE MURDERS

CALL   **MILDRED WALLACE**   **DEBORAH SHEPPARD**

The front-page article I read on December 11, 2007 while home recovering from my accident. Reprinted with permission of the *St. Louis Post-Dispatch*, copyright, 2007.

'It's sad he ever got out'

By Jeremy Kohler
ST. LOUIS POST-DISPATCH

Confessions of a lifelong sex offender solved a series of murders in southeast Missouri, but left one mystery unsettled:

Why was Timothy Krajcir, with a long and violent rap sheet, repeatedly freed from prison decades ago, allowing him to commit more crimes?

In 1963, Krajcir, then 18, pleaded guilty to a rape and an attempted murder in the Chicago area. He was stationed at the Great Lakes Naval Training Center.

He also admitted to attacks, or attempted attacks, on 16 other women in Illinois and burglaries of 19 homes in Pennsylvania. He was sentenced to 25 to 50 years in prison.

Krajcir
Deemed a 'sexually dangerous person' in 1979

But he got out in 1976.

In 1979, he was convicted in Jackson County, Ill., of indecent liberties with a minor — akin to statutory rape. He was deemed a "sexually dangerous person," meaning he would be committed until he could prove to authorities that he had been rehabilitated.

But he was paroled in just two years, over the objections of John Clemons, then Jackson County state's attorney.

During the months when he was not imprisoned in the late 1970s and early 1980s, Krajcir murdered six women in Illinois and Missouri, police said Monday, and he has admitted three other slayings.

"It's sad he ever got out," said Carbondale Police Lt. Paul Echols on Monday. "But the judge was basing his decision on the Illinois Department of Corrections, which was in support of releasing him. The psychologists felt they could let him out."

This was the way things were in the 1970s, said David Zlotnick, a professor at Roger Williams School of Law in Bristol, R.I., and an expert in judicial sentencing.

"It was sort of the pinnacle of the rehabilitative approach to sentencing," he said. "We'd give them a long sentence, but allow a parole board to release them early with incentives to behave well in prisons and rehabilitate themselves. The problem is they didn't do such a good job of it in some places and it led to what we have today, a very punitive and nonrehabilitative approach to sentences."

Authorities then might not have been as tough on rapists as they would be now, he said. Rape was treated more like a property crime than one of violence.

Krajcir enrolled at Southern Illinois University Carbondale and graduated in May 1982 with a degree in administration of justice.

He moved back to Pennsylvania that July, and was charged with rape in Allentown that December.

He spent five years in prison for the assaults and for an unsuccessful attempt to break out of jail in May 1983. He was transferred back to Illinois in 1988 for violating parole, and has been in custody ever since.

It is possible, Echols said, that Krajcir could have convinced another parole board that he was ready to be released. He described Krajcir as smart, deceitful and persuasive.

But Krajcir decided long ago that he wanted to stay in prison, where he couldn't cause more harm.

That he chose to stay "might be to his own credit," Echols said.

jkohler@post-dispatch.com | 314-340-8337

MURDERS | FROM A1

Confession solves series of slayings

○ slayings of five women in Cape Girardeau in 1977 and 1982. Earlier in the day, he pleaded guilty in the murder of a college student in Carbondale, Ill.

Authorities have also charged Krajcir, 63, in a 1982 rape in Cape Girardeau and say he has admitted to three other murders in three other jurisdictions. Officials declined to release details on those crimes while authorities seek charges.

Krajcir confessed to the crimes and agreed to a plea giving him life in prison after detectives confronted him with DNA evidence linking him to one case.

He told a detective he was sorry about the crimes, but added, "I don't think the way you do. If I thought the way you do, I wouldn't have done it."

The string of seemingly random murders began in April 1977, when Mary Parsh, 58, and daughter Brenda Parsh, 27, were found shot dead in their home.

Later that year, Sheila Cole was abducted from a Wal-Mart parking lot. Her body was found the next day at an Illinois rest stop about six miles away. The 1974 graduate of Lindbergh Senior High School had been shot with the same kind of gun used to kill the Parshes.

Nothing for more than four years — coinciding with a time Krajcir was in prison for other crimes.

"I can't begin to tell you how frustrated we were," Gerecke said. "I would get up at 2 and 3 in the morning because I couldn't sleep. And I remember staring out the window, smoking cigarettes, asking 'Why can't we solve these homicides.'"

The crimes began again in January 1982. A woman was attacked, sexually assaulted in front of her 10-year-old daughter and bound like other victims, though she survived. A few weeks later another woman, Margie Call, 57, was found strangled in her home not far from the Parsh home and the Wal-Mart. She had been sexually assaulted.

About six months later, Mil-

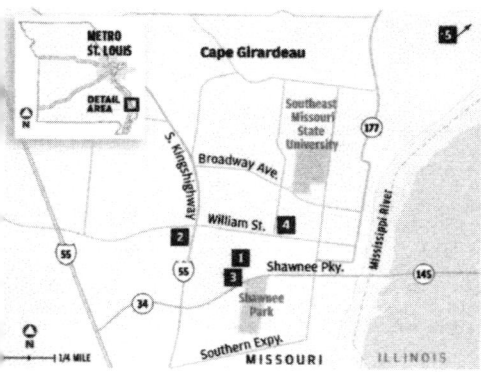

AREA MURDER VICTIMS

1 Mary and Brenda Parsh:
The bodies of Mary, 58, and her daughter, Brenda, 27, were found **Aug. 12, 1977,** in their home on Koch Street. The bodies were facedown, side-by-side on a bed, with their hands tied behind their backs. Each was shot once in the back of the head with a .38-caliber handgun.

2 Sheila Cole:
The 21-year-old student at Southeast Missouri State University was abducted from the parking lot of a Wal-Mart on South Kingshighway on **Nov. 16, 1977.** Her body was found the next day in a roadside restroom along Illinois Highway 3, near McClure. She had been shot twice in the head with a .38-caliber handgun.

Post-Dispatch

3 Margie Call:
The 57-year-old was found inside her home on Brink Street on **Jan. 27, 1982.** She had been strangled to death. She was found lying facedown on her bed with her hands folded across her back.

4 Mildred Wallace:
The 65-year-old was found in her home on William Street on **June 21, 1982.** She was shot once in the head with a .38-caliber handgun. She was found lying facedown on her bed.

5 Deborah Sheppard:
The 23-year-old Southern Illinois University student was found on the floor of her Carbondale apartment on **April 8, 1982.** She had been strangled and also suffered blows to the head.

...ed Wallace, 65, was found shot death in her home, also on the ...uth side of Cape Girardeau. She ...d also been sexually assaulted. ...e same year a Southern Illinois ...niversity Carbondale student ...as found dead in her apartment ...ere.

Then the murders stopped ...ain, just as Krajcir returned to ...ison for a parole violation in ...inois.

The break in the murder cases ...me 25 years later when Krajcir ...as arrested in August in the ...urder of the Carbondale stu-...nt, Deborah Sheppard, 23. The ...ld case was cracked by Lt. Paul ...hols of the Carbondale Police ...epartment, who sent previ-...sly untested evidence to a state

crime lab. DNA technology, not widely available at the time of Sheppard's 1982 murder, linked Krajcir to the crime.

Meanwhile, Cape Girardeau Police Detective Jimmy Smith had been assigned cold cases there. He noticed similarities between his cases and the Sheppard murder and contacted Echols.

They found that Krajcir had been to Cape Girardeau around the time of the crimes. And last month, after DNA tests and a palm print linked Krajcir to Wallace's death, they went to see Krajcir.

Investigators believed they had him on the murder of Wallace. Perhaps Krajcir thought so too.

So Krajcir offered a deal: Take

the death penalty off the table and he would reveal details about the murders of at least eight other victims.

Initially Cape Girardeau County prosecutor Morley Swingle balked at the idea but asked detectives to see what Mildred Wallace's family would want.

Teresa Haubold, 58, of Cape Girardeau, is Wallace's closest remaining family member and has served as the family's representative.

"It would be selfish to end (our case) and not bring closure to those other families," she said of the family's decision to OK the deal. "We never thought of it as anything special because we knew they would do that for us."

Smith and Echols met again with Krajcir on Dec. 3, this time with a letter in hand from the prosecuting attorney agreeing to waive the death penalty should he reveal details in the other murders. They got the confessions.

Echols said Krajcir has told him he is "twisted" and has been all his life. The investigator described Krajcir as "quiet-spoken, easygoing and very smart."

He's outwardly likable and people who have known him through the years are shocked to learn what he did, Echols said. Krajcir earned a degree from SIUC in administrative justice, the kind of degree someone going into law enforcement might get. Sheppard would have received a degree the same year, had she not been murdered a month before graduation.

Monday morning, Krajcir pleaded guilty in Murphysboro, Ill., to Sheppard's murder and was sentenced to 40 years, the maximum for murder at the time of the crime. Then authorities in Cape Girardeau announced the charges there: five counts of murder and three of rape.

"Some thought this had been forgotten, and it hasn't been forgotten," Smith said. "I remember the day I was notified that we had a possible DNA match. It was the most exciting thing that could ever happen to me."

After the announcement, Smith gave single white roses to the family members of victims who had come for the announcement.

"I'm glad it's over," he said as he gave Haubold a rose and the two embraced.

Terry Hillig of the Post-Dispatch contributed to this report.

cbyers@post-dispatch.com | 636-500-4106

Marion woman found s

Williamson County authorities today investigated the death of Mrs. Virginia Witte, 51, who was found stabbed to death in her home at 208 Lakeview Drive in Westernaire Estates in West Marion Friday afternoon.

Officers were summoned to the home after Mrs. Witte's husband, David, found her body lying on a bed with a kitchen knife in the lower portion of the left side of her chest.

Witte had left the house at 11:30 a.m. and his wife had gone to a grocery store at the same time. The couple had returned to Marion only the day before from a visit in Colorado. Investigators learned that when Witte returned to the home Friday about 1:15 p.m. he found that Mrs. Witte had arrived home ahead of him and the groceries she had purchased were on a counter in the kitchen. In a bedroom he found her dead, apparently from being stabbed with a knife taken from a kitchen cabinet drawer. The unclothed body bore the mark of several knife slashes across the abdomen, according to Coroner James R. Wilson who ordered an autopsy. The coroner said there was indication that Mrs. Witte had been strangled prior to being stabbed.

Witte, former district manager for General Motors Corp. and more recently operating his own investment firm, put in a call for the police.

Officers from the Marion police department, sheriff's office and the county detective unit and an ambulance responded. The house was sealed off while officers spent several hours in an on-the-scene investigation and questioning neighbors as t

The composite drawing published on Friday, May 19, 1978 on the front page in the local Marion, Illinois newspaper. The former parole officer to Timothy Krajcir saw this and reported that a former parolee of his could be this person. Courtesy of the *Marion Daily Republican*.

ɔbbed to death in home

vhether anyone had been seen leaving the Witte house.

Chief Deputy Sheriff Keith Odom said that no definite leads had been found, but said that interviewing of persons living in the area was continuing in the hope of finding a clue to the identity of the killer.

Although Odom said he did not go inside the house where detectives were conducting the investigation, it was reported that the house did not show signs of being ransacked, and that some valuable jewelry owned by Mrs.

Witte had not been taken.

Officers said there was no indication of forcible entry to the home.

The investigation was being continued today by the sheriff's office in cooperation with the county detective unit, Odom said.

Mrs. Witte was born in St. Louis August 6, 1926, the daughter of James and Leona Hilke Jokerst. She was married to David F. Witte at Webster Grove, Mo. June 4, 1947.

Besides her husband she is survived

by two sons, David F. Witte, Jr., Jefferson City, Mo., and Michael D. Witte, Denver, Colo. a granddaughter Monica Lee Witte, Denver, and two brothers, Charles Jokerst, LaFayette, La., and Norman of Walnut Creek, Calif.

She was a member of St. Joseph's Catholic Church where funeral services will be held Monday at 10 a.m. by Fr. Edward Balestrieri.

The Rosary will be recited at 7:30 p.m. Sunday at the funeral home where visitation will be after 4 p.m. Sunday.

The lead story in the local paper was the death of my neighbor, Virginia Lee Witte on Saturday, May 13, 1978. Courtesy of the *Marion Daily Republican*.

A picture of my two children that spring, 1978, playing in the backyard. A tree, with a useful notch, and the sandbox are just to the left of the picture.

Seek man reported near

The article that was published on the day of Virginia Witte's funeral, Monday, May 15, 1978. It provides information from an interview by police of neighbor Connie Clark, third paragraph from the end. Also, the article notes composite pictures she helped to devise, which afterwards were shown to me before publication. Courtesy of the *Marion Daily Republican*.

While funeral services were being held today for Mrs. Virginia Witte, 51, of Westernaires Estates a spokesman for the sheriff's office in a press conference at the Williamson County Courthouse said that preliminary results of an autopsy indicated death was due to a combination of choking, slashing of the abdomen and a stab wound in the chest. A man seen near the Witte home is being sought.

Sheriff's Detective William Henshaw said an extensive investigation is continuing into the death of Mrs. Witte who was found dead on a bed in her home at 1:05 p.m. Friday by her husband, David.

Standing in the county law library in the courthouse with Michael Wiseman, director of the County Detective Unit, Henshaw read a prepared statement as follows:

"On May 12, 1978, at approximately 1:05 p.m., the Williamson County Sheriff's Department received a telephone call from Mr. David Witte of 208 Lakeview Drive. Mr. Witte stated that he needed the police and an ambulance at his residence, because he thought his wife had been murdered.

"Uniformed police officers arrived at the scene at approximately 1:15 p.m., followed by investigative personnel at approximately 1:20 p.m.

"Upon arriving at the scene, the body of the victim, Virginia Witte, age 51, was observed. The body of Mrs. Witte was nude and lying on the bed of her bedroom. Initial observation revealed Mrs. Witte had received a large wound across the abdomen, which appeared to be a slash caused by a knife. Mrs. Witte also had a knife protruding from her chest. Clothing from the body was located near and about the bed.

"Further investigation was began by the Marion Police Department, Williamson County Detective Unit, and the Williamson County Sheriff's Department.

"The body was removed and taken to the Herrin Hospital where an autopsy was performed by Dr. AS Thompson, residence pathologist.

"Complete details of the autopsy was

tributable to a combination of choking the slashing of the abdomen, and th stab wound in the chest. Time of deat was established to be around 12:0 noon.

"A man was observed at the Witt residence near the time of death. It i not known at this time if the individua observed was the person responsibl for Mrs. Witte's death or a friend wh may have stopped by. All possible lead are being followed, attempting to gai the identity of this individual.

"During the investigation more tha one-hundred items of possible evidence were removed from the crime scene These items will be examined by th FBI Laboratory to determine thei evidential values."

"An extensive investigation i presently under way in an attempt t apprehend the individual responsibl for the death of Mrs. Witte."

Henshaw and Wiseman answere questions from reporters in the pres conference. Henshaw said a verba report on the autopsy was expected in day or two and that a detailed writte report was anticipated within a week.

He said that a man seen driving in the vicinity of the Witte home Frida was being sought in the investigation He said the man was reported to hav been seen by several persons, but tha descriptions varied and further infor mation is being sought. From bits of in formation received by residents of th neighborhood he said the man wa believed to be 30 to 40 years old and o muscular build.

Two composite pictures have bee placed in the hands of law enforcemen agencies for assistance in identifying the man sought. Wiseman said that whil the pictures vary in detail, they repre sent witnesses recollection of the sam man. A more accurate picture of th man actually seen in the neighborhoo is expected to be placed in circulation on the basis of later bits of description he said.

Witnesses interviewed, Henshaw said, told officers the man was driving a late model car. It was learned that some described it as a silver or white

86

urder scene

struggle in the bedroom where Mrs. Witte's body was bound, Henshaw said the nearest thing to evidence of a struggle was in the kitchen where Mrs. Witte's purse was found on the floor.

Examination of the kitchen indicated he had put away some of the groceries she had bought before her return home, and some remained in sacks.

Her clothing found in the bedroom had not been torn.

Asked if the victim had been sexually assaulted, Henshaw said determination would have to await the autopsy report.

To a question as to whether robbery had been ruled out, Henshaw said that valuable jewelry owned by Mrs. Witte had not been taken, and her husband could find nothing missing from the home, but since a motive has not been determined, robbery has not been ruled out.

Asked if officers had received a report from one mother living near the Witte home that she became so alarmed at the presence of a stranger who stopped there that she called her children into the house and locked the door, Henshaw replied that officers had talked to several women in the neighborhood but did not obtain information that any of them had talked with the stranger.

One newsman asked Henshaw why the coroner was not notified of the murder until two hours after the body was discovered, and the detective said it was his responsibility to call the coroner, and that he was busy collecting evidence inside the house up until the time the coroner was called. Wiseman said he did not believe the call was delayed two hours.

Henshaw said it was believed the murder weapon was taken from a cabinet in the kitchen of the home.

Attending the press conference but not taking part were Sheriff Russell Oxford and Chief Deputy Keith Odom.

Undated picture of Virginia Lee Witte given to me from the case file of the Marion police department.

The intersection of Skyline and Lakeview Drives, looking east toward our house. The Witte house is on the immediate left. The Clark house is across the street on the right hand corner. Our house is the third on the left—the planting area where I was working when Krajcir drove up is noted by the arrow.

The Clark house—Connie was mowing in this area when I made my run into my house to retrieve my gym bag. Also, this was approximately where she saw Krajcir make his second pass by her house.

The Witte house, view from my mailbox across the road. The bump-out was a front bedroom which Virginia may have used primarily as her own and where the sexual assault began. The master bedroom where she died is at the rear of the house, not visible.

A picture of the Patterson house as it appeared the year we moved in, 1978.

Front view of the Patterson house.

March 16, 2008 photo of Lieutenant Paul Echols, Carbondale, Illinois police department, left, and Detective Jimmy Smith of the Cape Girardeau police on the right. Reprinted with permission of the *St. Louis Post-Dispatch*, copyright 2008.

Marion, Illinois Detective Christina Morrow, who served as lead detective in resolving the cold-case murder of Virginia Witte. She is giving a statement after the guilty plea from Tim Krajcir at the Williamson County Courthouse or Friday, January 18, 2008. Courtesy of the *Southern Illinoisan*, photographer Steve Johnke.

Timothy Wayne Krajcir being escorted by his security detail into the federal courthouse in Cape Girardeau, Missouri on Friday, April 4, 2008. Entered a guilty plea that would brand him as both a serial killer and rapist and ensure he would never be out of prison again. Reprinted with permission of the *St. Louis Post-Dispatch*, copyright 2008.

91

the daughter in the head, shot the mother in the head and put a blanket over their heads, left to go get cleaned up. The mother thought he was gone. She started to cry so he went back and shot her again. If she would've been able to lie there long enough she would've been able to provide a description of the killer."

Per Krajcir, "I heard her crying and I guess she thought I was gone." He did not want to leave a witness. She had seen his face.

Normally for his sexual assaults he wore a blue bandana over his face. The elderly women he assaulted did not try to pull the bandana down. With Virginia Witte, he did not wear a bandana.

Me: "He was very bold." I was referring to the somewhat atypical case with Virginia Witte.

Detective Morrow: "He came in broad daylight with the intent to kill."

We discussed his claim that he followed Virginia home from the grocery store. I pointed out that Connie saw him driving around the block at least three times. I saw him on Monday of that week driving the same route she described, in reverse.

Detective Morrow said that during the interview Lieutenant Echols tried to get him to pinpoint exactly where the house was. His methods were to pick out a victim, follow her home, and know where she lived, whether she lived alone or not. He knew things about his victims. He would return later, prepared to carry out the crimes as dictated by his fantasies.

He scouted, or "hunted" neighborhoods and parking lots.

I wonder if just following her home from the grocery store would have sufficiently familiarized him with the area.

I asked her if, when they were looking at any of these cases, was there "any thread that would have linked any of these crimes together?"

"With the sexual assaults and later on a couple of murder victims, we did have the type of cord, or rope used to tie the victims. All were tied. He could use whatever was at hand, but liked a type of boot lace he carried in his pocket. Same type of naval knot. A lot of times he used the blue bandana. He was usually in the house, at night."

Me: "He could do breaking and entering?"

Detective Morrow: "Absolutely. He would steal; take money out of their purse."

I mentioned that some small comfort after the Witte murder was that this was a man looking for an easy entry into a home, and that if we kept our doors and windows locked, we might be all right. Now, I found out differently.

Detective Morrow: "He has given enough details of this crime (the Witte murder) that, after having spoken with him, he has to have had direct knowledge."

Me: "It seems like there were just certain times he had a need, a compulsion to kill someone. I really think he came to our subdivision with that intent that day."

Detective Morrow: "I tend to agree with you. There were things he had difficulty remembering. He said, 'I was frantic, I was in a hurry'."

And also, he mentioned he 'was lucky her husband didn't come home' while he was there."

Maybe Virginia had told him her husband would soon be home and that is why he was in kind of "a hurry".

Krajcir was asked what he did after Virginia's murder. He said he just gathered his things and left. He did not clean up, but did not feel the need to. Per the coroner, lack of significant blood loss probably meant her heart had dramatically slowed or stopped beating. So, he might not have had much blood splatter to clean off.

He mentioned people had seen him, saying, "One lady was out mowing, and another was out, doing things around her house. They saw me pull up."

Krajcir was out of his comfort zone; he was much more a creature of the night. And in fact, he never again returned to crimes during the daylight hours.

We discussed a *St. Louis Post-Dispatch* article I had with me. It pictured Krajcir and some old black and white photos of his murder victims displayed underneath his color photo. I stated I had found this "deeply disturbing". His victims were almost like a "footnote" to his story, and that bothered me.

Detective Morrow said after a court appearance she had stressed to reporters who wanted to ask questions that it was a day of justice for Virginia Witte and her family. She is survived by two sons. Her husband is deceased.

Me: "Does he think the woman got what they deserved?"

Detective Morrow: "No, he never said that."

Me: "So, it's all about him?"

Detective Morrow: "Him and his own compulsions. He was very matter-of-fact. Did this, and while I was there, I did this and this and this. He would go through the details of committing the crimes like he was reading a book."

Sometimes a flash of reality would dawn on him. They showed him crime scene photos, Lieutenant Echols throwing them down on the table while asking Krajcir about them.

Rubbing his forehead, he said, "Those are very disturbing pictures."

Me: "Does he have any regrets?"

Detective Morrow: "No. Not really. For the victims or for the families."

She went on to say, "He may have thought this would be some sort of catharsis for him, but it is extra burdensome to him now."

As a sexually dangerous person he was able to stay in prison. He told detectives when he was out of jail he had a tendency to hurt people, so he wanted to stay in jail.

When Lieutenant Echols re-submitted DNA from Deborah Sheppard's case, the new technology brought up a match with Krajcir's DNA.

Having discovered a newly-designated serial killer, the police departments are playing "catch-up" to what he had already admitted to having done.

Also, he has been moved to a more secure facility. He has little contact with others. He is on permanent lock-down. All his "little freedoms" he had before in prison are gone. He is considered a danger to other inmates and in danger from them as well.

And danger lurks not only in the prison system for him now. A tactical team is mobilized for any court appearances or movement. Even though there are still justifiably angry relatives out there, Krajcir has received death threats from *other* dangerous people wanting to make a name for themselves by murdering a serial killer.

So, Krajcir feels safer in prison than out. And there, he is at least "free" from acting on his own compulsions.

But, Detective Morrow says, "Now I don't want anybody to think that he is trying to rehabilitate himself. I don't believe that to be the case. He doesn't claim to be in a rehabilitative state. He isn't trying to make it all right with God. He doesn't have that mindset."

And, "Lieutenant Echols prompted him to give some closure for the victim's families, not for the victims themselves."

According to Detective Morrow, the police at the time put a huge effort into this investigation. As she pointed out, this was before commonly used forensic procedures of today. Old-fashioned detective work involved a lot of knocking on doors, to which I can attest. I knew they had spent a lot of time inside the house gathering evidence. And I have seen the containers that hold the case file.

"If they hadn't laid that ground work and put all these things together, including interviewing in the neighborhood and talking to car dealerships and putting together a case file, all this stuff wouldn't matter. The confession is just as good as the credible evidence that goes behind all of it. The confession would have been worthless. He knows the evidence is there."

I asked her, what, to her, was the most shocking thing about all these cases.

She replied, "His complete lack of emotion. He has no emotion for the things he has done and the heinous nature of, well, Virginia's case, for starters. Slashing somebody and leaving their stomach open, you know, to me that is pretty heinous."

" And to kill a mother and daughter and realize, oops, I missed and then go back without any remorse and make sure you did the job a second time and then not have any additional remorse for that—'Oh, she was whimpering and crying, so I realized she wasn't dead so I went back and I shot her.' Just like you are reading a grocery list."

"That's probably the most shocking thing, that he just didn't— everything was so matter-of-fact."

So, Virginia Witte's case was a departure from Krajcir's usual comfortable (for him) and successful methods. He was not masked and therefore police thought he had most likely come to our neighborhood that day with the intent to kill.

However, to think he had abandoned completely his "hunting" methods seems too atypical. After all, I did see him face-to-face, stopping and checking the street signs on the corner. Plus, with Connie's statements, both voluntarily and under hypnosis, we know that he was circling the block prior to Virginia arriving home. Krajcir was not also sitting on a parking lot at the same time. He could not have followed her home, as he was already in the subdivision, intently and urgently seeking his next victim.

Additionally, Virginia's schedule was not typical on that day. They had been gone to Colorado for several days, and had only just returned the prior evening. She had worked until they left on their vacation. Her husband, although out for his luncheon meeting, was retired and normally home during the day and evening. David Witte was not an elderly man like in the other husband-and-wife couples Krajcir victimized, but a robust and young retiree.

Per Connie's statement, he seemed to be "looking for someone". Also, the statement Connie gave while under hypnosis indicated Krajcir actually got out of his car and looked every direction before pulling into the driveway. It would seem he made up his mind at the last minute. Perhaps Virginia was not the intended victim, but the person he "found". The killer himself seems somewhat vague on a few of the details, so we may never know.

It was nearly thirty years ago, and he has committed many, many crimes.

Chapter Nine

Lieutenant Paul Echols,
Carbondale, Illinois Police Department

January 30, 2008

L ieutenant Echols and I talked for about an hour. In late 2007, he had gotten the ball rolling when he broke the 1982 "cold case" murder of SIU college student Deborah Sheppard. He was able to obtain a DNA match and take this evidence to Krajcir at the Big Muddy Correctional Center in Ina, Illinois in late 2007.

According to Detective Morrow, who was with Echols during some of the interviewing, he began by placing this case before Krajcir, saying he had witnesses who had seen him at the murder scene. This Krajcir denied. All the while, Echols had new DNA evidence in his "back pocket", but he wanted to see what Krajcir had to say before revealing this.

After the suspect realized there was concrete evidence against him for murder charges, he was willing to bargain. Krajcir wanted the death penalty removed, and then he would talk to law enforcement officials. Up until this time, no murder charges had ever been filed against him.

Krajcir had had years to think about this eventuality. He even remarked at one point to detectives that he wondered why no one had knocked on his door about some of his unsolved crimes before then.

During the visits between Krajcir and Lieutenant Echols, more breakthroughs occurred. Lieutenant Echols worked hard to develop a rapport with this killer. His approach, he said, was to appeal to Krajcir to give closure to the families.

Krajcir has told him he doesn't "think like you do or I never would've done it". And, he further states that he has been "twisted" all his life.

Lieutenant Echols says Krajcir does not feel any remorse. This was reinforced by Detective Christina Morrow in Marion. Once it is done, it is over. He went to a wedding the day after he assaulted and killed the Parsh women, mother and daughter, one of his most heinous crimes, and appeared just fine. He probably felt fine, too. He was free, at least temporarily, of the compulsions that drove him.

Lieutenant Echols kindly emailed me the newspaper accounts of the local Marion headlines from the Witte murder. I remembered reading them, vaguely. Local papers, plus the local television news—coverage was all but inescapable. Krajcir said he did not particularly follow this coverage, and in fact, he rarely knew or bothered to find out the names of his victims. His remarkable memory as to dates, times, places and methods have assisted the police in matching his confessed crimes to his victims.

Lieutenant Echols showed him the composite sketch that Connie Clark worked on, and he said "That doesn't look like me." He mentioned he lacked that much hair! If he had seen the sketch previously in any of the local newspapers, he had either forgotten it, regarding it as unimportant, or ignored it completely at that time.

Echols had re-interviewed Krajcir on January 29, in his new prison, the Tamms Correctional Facility. Tamms is a State of Illinois maximum security prison located on the Illinois side of the Mississippi River, about 17 miles from Cape Girardeau, Missouri and about thirty miles from Carbondale. Krajcir's designation from sexually dangerous person has been upgraded to that of a serial killer, thus the change to a supermax facility. Per Lieutenant Echols, the FBI defines this as a murderer of two or more persons.

Perhaps the FBI will become more involved with Krajcir and do a profile, eventually. Besides closure for the remaining family members and justice for the surviving victims, (no small thing) perhaps learning more about what makes this individual tick will help in the future with better crime solving capabilities. Perhaps earlier and better identification of individuals prone to sick violence or those that cannot, or have not, been helped by therapy will be the next huge scientific advancement.

I was beginning to understand that dark compulsions had irresistibly ruled Krajcir's life. I could not understand how he was not prominently on the police "radar".

I asked Lieutenant Echols if Krajcir had not had run-ins with the law while he lived in Carbondale. It seemed hard to believe he had not come to the attention of law enforcement officials while living there right under their noses.

There were a couple of instances of exposing himself to children, he replied. This occurred while still on parole as a convicted sex offender. It was not deemed sufficient to revoke his parole and send him back to prison, but was looked upon as a form of decompression, a release, that hopefully meant he would not reoffend with something worse. Lieutenant Echols reflected that at that time of the Witte murder he "did not think Krajcir was even still on parole."

Krajcir supported himself working as an EMT and later was absorbed in a company merge into an ambulance crew. Echols thought his status as an ex-offender was known. He had earned his EMT license in prison. He has the impression that Krajcir was well-regarded for his skill and competency by fellow workers. He is credited with saving lives while on the job, and even delivering a couple of babies.

With an IQ in the 120 to 130 range, Krajcir would probably have seemed to be intelligent, diligent and well-trained while on the job. But he could not resist the compulsions that drove him. His "dark side", as Lieutenant Echols refers to it, emerged and triumphed time after time. Krajcir feels he could probably have gotten another release from prison if he had desired it. Having been released before, he knew that if he went to the counseling provided, at some point he could once again have been deemed "cured" and released. He refused the counseling and thus had remained in prison until the murder charges have been brought against him.

Krajcir has referred to himself as "out-of-control" to various people when not in prison. His compulsions seem to be so great and relentless to "hunt" new victims that seemingly he did not want out again.

He was sent back to prison while in Carbondale after having been convicted of sex with a minor. Two daughters of his landlord, the older child only 11, had possibly developed a crush on Krajcir. He took full advantage for two years, until she turned 13 and the father found out and notified police. He was sent back to Menard Psychiatric facility in Chester, Illinois.

I asked if Krajcir was able to have or maintain a normal relationship with a woman. Lieutenant Echols said Krajcir was briefly married, living in northern Illinois, but it only lasted weeks or a few short months. He was actively raping women while in the marriage. Short as the marriage was, it did produce a daughter. He had a girlfriend of sorts while in Carbondale, but it was more of a friendship than a relationship, he felt.

The real turn-on for him apparently was the power and domination of the sexual act with a non-consenting woman. Lieutenant Echols said he was more or less impotent in a mutual sexual situation. Oral sex was very important to him.

"Giving, or receiving?" I asked.

"Both," Echols replied.

Krajcir was a total package. He was a thief with breaking-and-entering skills who would lie in wait for his victims to come home after he had "hunted" them and planned his crimes. He stole from his victims if they had something he wanted after he finished sexually assaulting them.

He came into possession of firearms this way and also from breaking-and-entering. The gun Krajcir used to murder Shelia Cole and the Parsh women, and linked by ballistic testing, was obtained during a burglary in Carbondale. In all, he used a gun to commit four murders. He cruised neighborhoods, and parking lots at grocery stores and Wal-Mart, and sometimes followed his would-be-victims home. He planned the best times to commit his crimes. He was highly organized. Once he even followed his victim home from church. Oh, yes, and he was a "Peeping Tom", too.

I asked Lieutenant Echols why Krajcir had chosen to murder some of his sexual assault victims, but not most of them.

He said in the case of college student Deborah Sheppard, Krajcir started out spying on her as the "Peeping Tom". He progressed to entering her home with the leather shoe laces in his pocket and his buck knife in hand. He was also wearing his blue bandana over his face. After the attack, Deborah grabbed the bandana and pulled it down. During prior prison time, a fellow inmate had given him this advice: Never leave anyone alive who can identify you. Krajcir told Lieutenant Echols he had not forgotten this.

Up until that point of the bandana being pulled down, he said he was pretty much done there. After Deborah yanked the bandana down, she had to die.

I asked if anyone who could identify him had ever been left alive.

"No," he replied.

I pointed out that statements made by the police to the press on information given them by Connie Clark, in particular, could have sufficiently alarmed him about the possibility of having left a witness to the Witte crime. Also, there were face-to-face meetings between Krajcir, Connie and myself, and who-knows-who-else might have sighted this man and put two and two together. Echols agreed it could have. I was glad we were not overtly interviewed or quoted in the press or interviewed on television, even though Krajcir said he had not been following the coverage all that intently.

He would have had to have known who Connie was, at least, if he read the papers. One article, titled "Seek man reported near murder scene" in the *Marion Daily Republican* on Monday, May 15, 1978, stated that after sighting him, "One young mother, sufficiently alarmed, called her children and went inside." Why the article did not continue to say she was the woman who lived across the street and saw the killer go into the Witte home, gave a description of his car and drew up a composite sketch identifying him, I don't know. He possibly could have come to our neighborhood, since he was so familiar with it, and finish off the people who had seen him up close.

We were all, I think, civilians and police alike, ignorant of the type of person we were dealing with. We were floundering, trying to do the right thing, or in the case of the police, cover as much ground as possible. None of the civilians perceived any danger to themselves. Nor were we cautioned by anyone in authority, except for that one time an officer mentioned to me to stay alert, because the killer might return to the crime scene "to gloat" as he put it.

And, actually, the composite was incorrect in a couple of areas. The hair pictured as full and neatly combed might, at least on top, actually have been a dark ball cap. Shown the sketch by Detective Morrow and Lieutenant Echols, he said, "That doesn't look like me." He indicated the lack of hair. He denied wearing a hairpiece, but did indicate that he had used a stocking cap a time or two and might have been wearing a dark ball cap.

If, in fact, he did wear a dark cap the day I saw him, it might have appeared as dark hair matching his mustache and what facial hair I could see clearly. It was a bright, sunny day, and he was inside the car. Toward the top of the vehicle, it would have been shaded. If the cap had been a brighter color, it would have stood out.

Also, the composite picture shows glasses. I did not indicate glasses, and in fact I stated that he did not have them. Connie's composite shows glasses, as she could not remember if he had been wearing glasses or sunglasses. Krajcir said he might have been wearing sunglasses.

Krajcir's eyes are officially listed as brown. Detective Morrow said they were more hazel. We had discussed how eyes with his coloration could change with clothing and lighting. In my statement to the police I indicated his eyes were light blue. They seemed that day to be a steely pale blue to me. My own son's eyes are changeable, too, so I know how different factors can come into play. I am comfortable with the statement as it is.

I asked Lieutenant Echols if he had read my statements, and gave him one or two Detective Morrow had produced from the files. I also showed him Connie's original statement and the statement they took while she was under hypnosis.

Because the police had had at the time some pretty definite information on the vehicle, they put out a massive info net to all car dealers for miles and miles. They were looking for a new or year-old silver two-door Chevy, and wanted to know who had purchased one. Krajcir was notified by the dealer he purchased the car from that the police might be contacting him in the future as they were asking the dealers for this information. His name appears on one of these lists in the case file in Marion, as verified by Detective Morrow as well as Lieutenant Echols.

As for gaining entry to the homes of his victims, besides breaking-and-entering and lying in wait, he sometimes pretended to be a delivery person. He would use a clipboard, or in the case of Virginia Witte, brought a box to the door and said he needed her to sign for a delivery. He told Echols that before he left, he took the box with him, not wanting to leave it behind for evidence. Of course, he had his buck knife when he knocked on her door. He did not have his blue bandana. He had no disguises at all.

Detective Morrow had earlier said to me, "Not to give you a warm and fuzzy feeling, but he came to your neighborhood to kill someone."

I asked Lieutenant Echols how others present during his crimes had fared, obviously besides his main targeted victim. This has been a recurring and personal question for me. My actions (or some might say, lack thereof) during my encounter with Krajcir were all geared toward the survival of my very young children.

His reply was along the lines of Detective Morrow's—that he used any children as "leverage." He used their continued safety to better his chances that the mother would feel compelled to do whatever he asked as a way of protecting her children. Lieutenant Echols further stated that he had "never harmed a child, usually putting them in another room. Once he even admitted to going to check on the children.".

In January, 1982, however, he did admit to sexually assaulting a woman in front of her 10-year old daughter, according to *the St. Louis Post-Dispatch*, Dec. 11, (December 11, 1982?) St. Charles Edition. Also, there was the 13-year old minor he had sex with in Carbondale.

And he could take a dim view if the mother tried to leave and see about her child. One case in Northern Illinois involved a Mother trying to go to her child. He stabbed her with a ten-inch pair of scissors, puncturing her lung and nearly killing her.

She survived, and he was convicted of the rape and attempted murder.

No one can argue that the children involved in encounters with Timothy Krajcir were harmed psychologically, if not necessarily bodily.

Echols says, oddly enough, that he believes Krajcir feels some "embarrassment" for the crimes themselves at this point. How astonishing. For a man that was only rarely out of prison to have had such a successful career as a criminal, I would think embarrassment would be the last thing he would feel. I, in fact, wonder if he can feel much of anything at all. His total lack of feeling is simply breathtaking. Just when you think sexual perversion and murder has become mundane, new things emerge. Both Detective Morrow and Lieutenant Echols have stated that his dark side knows very few bounds. Whatever he could think up, he would do.

For instance, the abduction of Joyce Tharp of Paducah, Kentucky was a different approach for him, much as the daytime murder and assault of Virginia Witte was a departure from his usual nocturnal activities. He admitted to traveling to Paducah, Kentucky, about 80 miles, sighting her in a parking lot, and following her home. He kidnapped her and brought her back to his trailer home in Carbondale where he assaulted her and killed her. He kept her body for two days inside the trailer before bundling her up and taking her back to Paducah. There he dumped her nude body behind a church. He has not said what he did with the body for those two days.

In every conversation I have had with a law enforcement official, the Parsh women have come up each time. This seems to stick in everyone's mind as one of Krajcir's most heinous crimes, and one I was as yet unfamiliar with. Krajcir followed Mary Parsh, 58, of Cape Girardeau, Missouri, home, returning later to lie in wait. Both Mary and her daughter, Brenda, 27, were killed. Apparently, the daughter had just arrived home for a visit and Krajcir had not seen her before. Brenda and Mary had arrived home from the local airport together. Brenda's father was in the hospital at that time and he wanted to see his daughter. Krajcir did not let an extra person deter him from his plans. Evidently he viewed this as a bonus.

But this time he had a gun that he had stolen from another victim's house after a robbery. Krajcir had not used his bandana because he had planned on leaving no witnesses alive who could identify him.

I was speechless at this point in our conversation. I could not imagine the terror and trauma this poor woman and her daughter suffered. In my own opinion, it would be a fate *worse* than death for any mother not to be able to protect her children. I would rather die trying, and perhaps this is just what Mary did, in whatever way was available to her.

As we were wrapping up our conversation, I stood up to gather some papers.

I mentioned to Lieutenant Echols that I was sure he had returned to our neighborhood after killing Virginia. I expressed my frustration that no one had responded in time to find him there, and there seemed to be no follow-up with me after my phone call.

He replied in an offhanded manner, "Oh, they had him."

I was astounded. I sat back down in the chair, and my jaw dropped.

"What do you mean?" I asked.

Besides the list from the car dealer, which his name appeared on, the police also received a call from his parole officer. Lieutenant Echols felt Krajcir was no longer on parole by the time he committed the Witte murder, but the parole officer, having read the newspaper accounts of the murder and having seen the police artist sketch published therein, called and said one of his parolees could be a suspect.

In response to this, the Marion police dispatched someone to Krajcir's trailer. He watched him come and go. He noted Krajcir's physical description and that of the car, which did match up with descriptions given by Connie Clark and me. A report was subsequently typed up which remains in the case file to this day. No one detained him and they did not question him. There is no notation from a detective in the case file, as would be the case if there was a follow-up of any kind. There remain in the permanent case file a few lonely pieces of paper mentioning Krajcir, specifically.

They just had so many other leads to follow.

Chapter Ten

Seeking Answers

That comment made by Lieutenant Echols towards the end of our conversation on January 30, 2008, had certainly stunned me. It continued to haunt my thoughts. Somehow, I always knew Krajcir's name had to have come up in the Witte investigation.

As I looked through the case files I had requested from the Marion Police Department via The Freedom of Information Act, I remembered my telephone call to Detective Morrow after that comment made by Echols.

She indicated that due to a contact from a parole officer, an intern or two was assigned to follow up this lead.

They did a pretty good job.

In the case files I noted there were fairly thick files in manila folders on several other suspects they were seriously trying to develop, but for some reason Timothy Krajcir just seemed to slip through every crack and crevice afforded him. Even with his record as a violent sexual offender he was never seriously put forth as a suspect, he was not questioned. The other suspects, for one reason or another, did not go anywhere after awhile.

An intern to the Williamson County Detective Unit, one John Speroni, was spot on. He is now the Honorable Judge John Speroni, an Associate Circuit Court Judge in Williamson County. I briefly spoke with the Judge between hearings in mid-May, 2008.

He says he was then a law school student, and after a summer internship with the County Detective Unit, was headed back to law school to finish his studies.

He remembers, barely, typing his reports. He said he never did go out to the field and do any of the interviewing or investigative work involved with the Witte case. He said he was pretty much a "warm body," doing what he was told to do. His reports remain part of the permanent case file today and have a thoroughness that reflects well on the young law student-to-become-judge one day.

Speroni typed a report on May 17, 1978 that covers a lot of territory. To begin with, he contacted Jack Jones, a then-recent parole officer for Timothy Krajcir. I was told by several sources that Krajcir was not actually on parole at the time of the Witte murder, and this seems to bear out. Mr. Jones had initially called them with concerns.

Speroni summarized the interview as follows:

"Jones (the Parole Officer) advised that Krajcir was a parolee to him and stated that Krajcir bore a remarkable resemblance to the composite drawing of the subject in the Witte case. Jones advised Krajcir was discharged from parole in January of 1978, and at the time of discharge, Krajcir had a pencil-thin mustache. Jones also advised that Krajcir was selling insurance for the Chicago based firm of Combined Insurance of America at that time."

It is hard to believe Krajcir got a job selling insurance. He was a convicted rapist, having also had attempted murder charges against him, had been arrested for indecent exposure, and burglarized like crazy. I guess they might not have done much in the way of a background check when he was hired.

The report goes on to say, "Jones stated that Krajcir's prison record was very good; he was considered a model inmate and was often allowed outside the prison on ambulance runs, during the later part of his prison term."

"Krajcir is currently employed by the Jackson County Ambulance Service and has a good work record."

He received his EMT training in prison at the Vienna, Illinois Correctional Center in southern Illinois, where he was transferred in December of 1972. Lieutenant Echols had stated that he thought the ambulances services in Carbondale, Illinois in

108

1978, knew his background when they hired him.

This was not the only report bringing the name of Timothy Krajcir forward. Another Williamson County Detective Unit's Investigative Memorandum typed on 5-18-78 and authored by Assistant State Attorney Steve Cullison stated:

"Purpose: To report information in regard to Timothy Krajcir." The case detective noted was Henshaw.

On May 15, 1978, about 6:30 in the evening, Steve Cullison drove by an address on North Springer Street in Carbondale, Illinois. "In the back yard, facing a side street is a house trailer."

"In front of the trailer was a new looking, gray or silver Chevrolet Nova, bearing '78 Illinois license #CR 2200. This number registers to Timothy Krajcir, but to a 1969 Dodge. I observed no stickers in the windows. There was a "Grob" decal (the car dealer in Murphysboro, Illinois where Krajcir purchased the car) on the trunk lid above the right rear tail light.

"As I drove by, I observed a subject walking from the car to the trailer. He was a white male, approximately six feet tall, muscular/athletic build, top of head bald with brown hair on sides and brown side burns. I had only a rear and side view of the subject and did not get a view of his face. He appeared clean shaven from the side. Subject was wearing dark pants, possibly jeans, and a football type blue and gold jersey, but without lettering or numerals."

The car and the physical description were a perfectly acceptable match to the descriptions both Connie and I had given to the police.

I was able to track down Mr. Cullison through another attorney. He is now in private practice in a town just east of Springfield, Illinois. He left Marion at the end of the year of the Witte murder, and felt the case at that time, "was winding down" without any new evidence coming to the fore. He remembers the case clearly, as he states this is the only murder case he was ever involved with.

He was more or less drafted to drive by the Carbondale address on his way home from work, as he then lived there. He dutifully submitted the above report as to his findings. He stated the investigation went on "24/7" for days. The investigators, of all stripes, met daily in the mid-afternoon in a little house just off the town square, close to the main police station. All new information was reviewed. He stated that it was an intense investigation and they even brought in as consultants members of other police forces, such as one at Southern Illinois University who had outstanding investigative credentials. He feels confident that they put forth a 100 percent effort to find the murderer and bring him to justice. At one point, the file was even taken up to Chicago for independent review, but he did not recall the agency that it was given to. Nothing further was recommended, he recalled.

One fairly interesting finding that came out of one meeting was the report that there were large numbers of past sex offenders in the area, particularly around Carbondale at that time. Mr. Cullison and the others working on the case were incredulous at the number of parolees serving as ambulance attendants in Jackson County. A big percentage of them had an EMT license. Whether or not any huge effort was made to sort through them and then do interviews as to their whereabouts on the day of the Witte murder is doubtful. Apparently it would have taken an army of interviewers.

The detectives, who had heard it all, were flabbergasted by this news. "You mean," one of them said, "that if I have a heart attack or need an ambulance in Jackson County, the crew that comes to get me are rapists and murderers?" Apparently, yes, for the most part. And one of them was named Timothy Krajcir.

And, as if the observation on May 15 by Assistant State's Attorney Steve Cullison was not enough to point to Krajcir as a suspect, then the report on May 16 by Special Agent Gary Ashman to Case Agent Evans from the Illinois State Police, presented on 5/21/78, should have raised all kinds of red flags.

He wrote: "On May 16, 1978, Grob Motors, Murphysboro, Illinois, was contacted and it was learned that Tim Krajcir purchased a 1978 Chevrolet Nova two door....on April 12, 1978. The vehicle was a special order....it was learned that Krajcir was employed by the Jackson County Ambulance Service."

"A confidential source employed at the Jackson County Ambulance Service, advised the reporting officer that he has never seen Tim Krajcir wear glasses or a wig. Further investigation determined that <u>Krajcir was not working Friday, May 12, 1978</u>. (The underlining is in the report.) The subject got off work

Thursday, May 11, at 6:00 p.m. and did not return to work until Saturday, May 13, 1978 at 6:00 p.m."

Several things strike me about this report: one, the activity was conducted four days after the murder, even though it was not typed and submitted until May 26. This was pretty quick work in the identification of the dealership that sold the car, and the investigator even learned the place of work of the suspect and pursued that, learning Krajcir was off the day of the murder. It was a wide net they cast to learn about the vehicle which included rental agencies, as well.

The fact that an investigator was out to his trailer in 24 hours is also pretty impressive. A good, promising, solid start, but other suspects were developed and pursued, while Krajcir was not. Krajcir was not even brought in for questioning, or for identification. Neither Connie nor I were asked to identify him from, say, the traditional line-up, or from a picture. As I recognized his picture in the newspaper as he appeared in the 1970s nearly thirty years later, I am positive I could have identified him then.

It also appears he was working nights at the ambulance service that week and was able to move about freely during the day to hunt, and kill, his next victim.

During my brief visit to obtain these new case file records and to speak with Judge Speroni, I had made arrangements to see Connie Clark. I wanted to share this new information with her. We met at her apartment and I watched for her reaction. She read quietly, and then lifted her left hand, as if to say "stop." She continued reading, riveted by what the case records were revealing. As the car checked out and the sighting with physical descriptions matched, and this information began to sink in, she was at first incredulous, then angry.

"They had him," she stated flatly. Pretty much what Echols had indicated, I told her.

During his confession to Lieutenant Echols and Detective Morrow he said he thought someone would talk to him about this murder, but no one showed up at his door. The car dealership had contacted him, saying information had been requested on people purchasing his type of vehicle, and that the police might want to talk to him.

Per Detective Morrow, his mention in the case file means he

was retained as a person of interest, but she does not know why he was not seriously developed as a suspect.

Again, a great beginning, but the momentum was lost somewhere.

Timothy Krajcir slipped through the cracks in the Witte case. And, the very best opportunity they would get to apprehend a newly-minted serial killer, had just slipped through the authorities' fingers.

PART THREE

JUSTICE AT LAST

Chapter Eleven

Timothy Krajcir Returns To Cape

Decmber 10, the day of my fall on the ice and concussion, was the first time I had heard of any breaks in cold cases, and the first time I had ever heard the name Timothy Krajcir. To be truthful, I cannot remember if I read it in the newspaper or heard it on the television, or probably both, that evening after I was released from the hospital. This is pretty fuzzy in my memory, but I immediately sensed a connection to the Witte case.

On January 3, 2008, another interview took place with Krajcir, this time at his new "home", the Tamms SuperMax Prison in Tamms, Illinois. As a now designated serial killer his accommodations have been upgraded, courtesy of the State of Illinois.

After having spoken with Detective Tina Morrow and Lieutenant Echols, I contacted Detective Jimmy Smith of Cape Girardeau. We talked and emailed. He kept me up-to-date on scheduled hearings, one of which was to be in Jackson, Missouri, the Cape Girardeau County Seat on March 13, 2008.

I decided to attend. As yet, I was fairly uninformed as to the events that had transpired in Cape Girardeau. That would soon change.

Some of the information regarding the crimes committed by Krajcir as detailed in court documents and police reports are disturbing. After much internal debate I have included a few of these details, both of the crimes in Cape Girardeau and in Williamson County, Illinois. I think it serves a couple of purposes; one, to highlight just who and what we are dealing with, and two, to illustrate how lucky Krajcir is to be drawing breath today. It is hard to envision anyone more deserving of the death penalty. But the compassion of the good people of Cape Girardeau for others who might not be able to obtain the closure they themselves were given except by Krajcir's confession spared him. It was a bargain with the devil, but it does seem that in the end, goodness really did triumph over evil. It took decades, but it finally happened.

The Office of the Prosecuting Attorney issued a press release at this initial hearing. Charges were brought to bear from sexual assaults in 1982, and a robbery of another woman and her husband in 1982, and outlined in Probable Cause statements. These new charges were the result of the "December 3, 2007" confessions to "Detective Jimmy Smith that he (Krajcir) had committed each of these crimes."

This first hearing dealt with five additional charges, four of them for the sexual assaults and one for robbery in the 1981 and 1982 time frame. In this particular robbery he got less than $150. He broke into the home of an elderly couple and robbed them at gunpoint. He was going to sexually assault the wife, but changed his mind.

The arraignment was held by video. He was not brought into the courtroom after having been transported from Illinois. It was thought that security would not be tight enough to bring him from across the street where he was being held in jail, to the courtroom. As an older courthouse, it may have been lacking some desired element for security, or it may have been too costly to assemble a team of U.S. Marshals to protect Krajcir. A security team is assembled to protect Krajcir wherever he goes.

Numerous other jailed inmates were paraded before the camera, and Judge Gary Kamp dispatched them one by one. Then the room was cleared, and Krajcir was brought in front of the camera, shackled hand and foot.

I had glanced down to take a note and when I looked back up, drew in my breath. All those years ago, Connie had worked hard on the police sketch. She had had the artist draw heavy glasses on the suspect, but I had disagreed with that, as the man I saw had not worn glasses.

Now he appeared with thick, black rubber prison-issued glasses, and except for the age difference, looked very much like that sketch.

Wearing the orange prison garb, Krajcir was polite, answering "Yes sir" to the Judge when he questioned him as to his understanding of the charges. As he was led away, he said, "Thank you."

The entire arraignment lasted about a minute. The judge found probable cause and Krajcir would now face additional charges. They would schedule another hearing for sentencing in early April.

Chapter Twelve

How Did We Get To This Point?

So, how *did* we get from point A to point B? And, to get to the heart of the matter, what was Krajcir doing out of prison at all?

Once again, my favorite intern to the Williamson County Detective Unit, John Speroni, had typed another report, dated 5-17-08 on Krajcir's activities. He had received a written communication from John Jones, Parole Agent, titled:

"RE: <u>Timothy Wayne Krajcir – Vienna - 1637</u> (This refers to Vienna Correctional Center and is probably his prisoner number while there.)

"Dear Detective Speroni:

Attached you will find the Statement of Facts and F.B.I. Sheet on above-named subject."

He concluded if he could be of further assistance to please contact him again, and attached documentation on Krajcir that went back to 1963.

These documents pertain to the hearing held on August 23, 1963, in Lake County, Illinois where he was being held on rape charges.

It lists his then address as Milwaukee, Wisconsin, birth date of November 28, 1944 in West Mahoney Township, Pennsylvania. His age was then 18. His Nationality was stated as Czechoslovakian-American. He was still in the Navy, and it lists his highest grade completed as tenth at this point. He was Protestant and married. Rather than having a jury trial, he pled guilty to charges against him.

The "Statement of Facts" is just that. It states the charges to which he is accused, the date he was indicted on these charges and the sentence he received. The date of Indictment was June 10, 1963, on a rape he committed February 27, 1963 in North Chicago. The details go like this: Krajcir, a sailor, was on leave and returning to Great Lakes Naval Training Station. He was on foot. He went to the home of a woman, J.T., and watched her through a window. She was in her nightgown, not surprising since it was about 11 p.m.

He decided to break into her house. On the back porch was a pair of grass cutting shears "with triangular blades of approximately six inches in length." He used these to force the door open and entered her home.

He encountered her outside the bathroom and said, "Be quiet. Don't look at my face. Remember your little baby in there; you don't want to see her face all cut up. You know what these would do to her face. Be quiet."

He grabbed her then, and she began to plead with him. He threatened her again. Then she was forced into the bedroom. Her nightgown buttoned at the front, and he opened the gown. He forced her onto the bed, lying with her gown opened. Again he warned her not to look at his face.

Apparently he had not yet met the street-wise mentor in prison who told him to never leave alive anyone who could identify him.

He demanded fellatio.

"Suck on it."

"Oh, God, please don't make me," she begged.

"Yes."

He then forced sexual intercourse on her.

All the while, he had not relinquished the shears with the six-inch triangular blades. He continued to hold the shears and run them up and down her legs while threatening her repeatedly.

After he left at about 12:22 a.m., she then called police at 12:40 a.m.

Additional evidence was presented for an April 10, 1963

crime at this hearing.

Krajcir broke into a house belonging to a Mrs. J.E. on Hickory Street in Waukegan, Illinois. He came through the back door, which was not locked. He walked right in and took off his shoes.

Mrs. E. was 27 and the mother of two. She thought she heard the door open, so she walked to the back of the house where she encountered Krajcir.

He said, "Cooperate and I won't hurt you and your baby." He made her go to the bedroom and tried to have sexual intercourse with her.

Her baby began to cry and she got up to go to him. Krajcir turned as if he was leaving, walked into the kitchen and found a pair of scissors with blades approximately 10 inches long. He went back to Mrs. E., and telling her not to look, stabbed her with the scissors in the back, puncturing her lung. He left her for dead. She was hospitalized for three weeks, but recovered.

Additionally, he testified at this hearing that he had committed four burglaries in Waukegan, one in North Chicago, and an additional 15 in Reading, Pennsylvania (where he is from) prior to joining the Navy.

He had been in the Navy less than a year, and was soon dishonorably discharged.

He also admitted "peeping" into windows of about two to three dozen homes in North Chicago and Waukegan and admitted on the stand that he masturbated while watching the women in them, seemingly safe, at least in their own minds, in their homes.

Psychiatrists submitted reports.

The defendant was sentenced to the Illinois State Penitentiary for the crime of rape "for not less than 25 years nor more than 50 years." The Judge also stated that Krajcir should "be removed from society."

For the 25- to 50-year sentence he received in June, 1963, Krajcir was held in jail in North Chicago, Illinois from May 8, 1963 on the charge of rape until he was transferred to Joliet State Prison on August 29, 1963. The "disposition" is stated at "25-50 years".

He was transferred from Joliet to Menard Penitentiary,

Psychiatric Facility, Illinois, on November 5, 1963. He stayed there until 1972. He was later to say that this was a terrible place. Various sources have told me that Krajcir probably had counseling here.

Deemed more or less "cured" he was sent to Vienna Correctional Center deep in the heart of the southern tip of Illinois for rehabilitative services. This is probably where he earned his EMT license, and he must also have completed his GED in prison along the way.

It is unclear from my research when he was released exactly from Vienna, but sometime early in 1977. He was able to purchase a new car in April of 1978, so he had a job and some money by then.

He had served about 14 years on a 25- to 50-year sentence, during which time he received counseling, education and job training and was good to go, a grad of the Correctional System of the State of Illinois.

Of course, the "lessons" he received from fellow inmates — the most important of these being to never leave a witness alive who could identify him and thus return him to prison, were not included on his transcripts.

He was free to start his life of crime in earnest. In 1977 alone, he has admitted to at least the following: burglaries in Carbondale, Illinois; April 12, attacked and killed Brenda and Mary Parsh; and the abduction and killing of Southeast Missouri State University student Shelia Cole in November that same year. He may have intended to kill the woman in northern Illinois when he stabbed her with the scissors, but at this time he became earnest about murder — deadly earnest.

He was off parole in January 1978, notwithstanding more than one occasion where he was caught exposing himself prior to this. These acts were not deemed sufficient to revoke his parole and send him back to prison.

But three murders, to which he had not yet confessed to having committed during this time frame, would certainly have earned him more than just a prison sentence. It would have meant the death penalty. It was something he and he alone, knew.

He must have felt emboldened, perhaps invincible. Krajcir rewarded himself with his custom-ordered new Chevy Nova in April, 1978; he came to our neighborhood the very next month.

I had no idea, even in my wildest imagination, that the man I looked up at, smiling as I kneeled planting my flowers on that beautiful spring day with my young children beside me, had such a dangerous past and destructive future and he was about to unfold it practically on my very doorstep.

At least not until Virginia Witte met her tragic, untimely death four days later.

Some of Krajcir's crime sprees within Williamson County included, in 1982, a series of rapes, robberies and home invasions targeting elderly people. 1982 was a prolific year for Timothy Krajcir. He committed three more murders and at least seven sexual assaults.

I obtained a couple of Investigative Reports on two of three of these known assault cases. None of the victims was younger than 65. I do remember reading about these incidents in the newspaper. However, no one, including the police, had any idea that these could be linked to the Witte case, or any other assault or robbery case in a neighboring town. All were considered local and in all probability, committed by someone known to the victims. By not tying these assaults together, Krajcir was once more getting more "stay out of jail cards."

Two of these victims, both women, are still living. Of the living, one is in declining health and according to police and relatives has remained fearful for the past 26 years, all due to Timothy Krajcir. In her early 90's now, she is not of very sound health.

On March 28, 1982, this lady, a widow then, was interviewed by Special Agent Greg Geittmann at the State Regional Office Building in Marion regarding "the burglary, robbery and deviate sexual assault."

She left home about 5:30 p.m. to go to church in the tiny town of Carterville, Illinois. Returning home about 7:30 p.m., she walked through the kitchen, pausing to take a bite or two of chicken. She then, according to the report, "walked through the living room and into the hallway…she turned the hallway light on and…removed her coat, preparing to hang the coat on the rack which was located in the hallway."

At this point, Krajcir, hiding in the next room, a bedroom, "dived at her."

He had a gun, which he pointed at her. She noted he held it in his right, not left, hand. She screamed, but Krajcir told her to stop, or he would "take care of her."

He took her eyeglasses and put her on her stomach in the hallway. He threw her coat over her head and tied her hands with heavy duty boot laces behind her back. He went through her purse and asked if she did not have more money.

She had some pennies in cups in the kitchen, she replied. He went to look, but did not find them.

He returned and pulled her dress up as she lay on the floor. Krajcir then pulled her pantyhose and panties down to her ankles. He asked her how old she was. He felt her buttocks, and "put his hand between her legs."

He asked her if she had "ever done it rectally; (and also) if she still got wet thinking about sex."

He asked for Vaseline. He asked when was the last time she had had sex, and if she enjoyed it.

He said he was going to rape her.

She said she needed to go to the bathroom, and asked to be untied.

He told her to get up and set her on the bathroom stool.

If she had been trying to get him to untie her, this ploy did not work. He soon pulled her up.

Krajcir unbuttoned her dress and pulled her bra down, commenting she had "pretty breasts." He then informed her "he was going to teach her things tonight she hasn't done before... (had) she ever licked a man's anus,...had (she) ever sucked anybody off."

He told her she "was going to suck him off. (She) stated the intruder forced her to get onto her knees. (He) then laid his pistol on the bathroom lavatory, unzipped his pants and played with his penis. (He) commented how pretty his penis was. (She) was forced to put her hands on his penis, and to masturbate him with her mouth...the intruder ejaculated and wouldn't let her vomit... the intruder kept her head forced down."

Krajcir then zipped his pants, telling her he was leaving. She was told to lie on the bathroom floor and not move for several minutes. After about five minutes, she peered into the hallway and got one hand free. She then walked out of the house and went to a neighbor's residence.

The intruder was described as a "white male, twenty or so and he wore a dark ski mask over his head. He also wore a surgical glove on his left hand. She did not recognize his voice, but said he seemed educated and soft-spoken using a pleasant tone. He did not appear to be nervous.

He also had not attempted sexual intercourse and did not insert his fingers into her body, nor did he strike her.

Krajcir got $45 cash from a terrified 65-year-old widow. When the police arrived at her home at about 8:17 p.m. that night she still had a cord around her right wrist and her dress was buttoned up wrong. He had gained entry through a back bedroom window. The neighbors never heard or saw anything unusual.

The police interview was interrupted when the victim had to vomit in the bathroom.

A little less than three months later, on June 6, 1982, police were called to the residence of an elderly couple. According to the Investigative Memorandum, the female victim was 70 years old, the male 73.

On a June night, the couple had been sitting on their back porch until about 9 p.m. They had gone inside, she to stretch out on the couch, and the husband disappeared into the front bedroom. They had not locked the back door.

The next thing she knew, a man was standing before her, in her own living room pointing a gun at her and yelling, "Hit the floor! This is a hold-up!"

The husband, hearing the commotion, came out of the front bedroom. Krajcir then made him lie on the floor, tied his hands behind his back and tied his feet. He put a coat over his head. He told the wife to lie across her husband.

At his confession to Detective Tina Morrow at the Big Muddy Correctional Center, he stated that he planned to sexually assault the wife as she lay across her husband.

But she refused, saying her husband had a heart condition and she would not do that. Her defiance would cost her. After ransacking a bedroom Krajcir asked her for her purse. He took whatever money was there and returned to the living room for the 70-year old wife. He took her to the bedroom, staying behind her the whole time. He entered her vagina from behind, ejaculating inside her. He then tried to enter her rectum, but she told him it "hurt too much".

His reply was that she would "either kiss his ass or suck his dick."

Still defiant, she said she would not kiss his ass.

The report continues, "He made her remove her teeth, put his penis in her mouth and told her to suck it. She stated he ejaculated in her mouth and on her face."

He then returned her to her husband, laying her across him, threatening to come back and kill them if they called police.

His haul, besides brutalizing an elderly couple in their 70's was a little over $1,000, plus a Social Security check for $64.80 and a .38 caliber Smith & Wesson snub-nose gun. The Social Security check might not have come in handy, but this man, Timothy Krajcir, could always make use of a snub-nose .38.

Chapter 13

Probable Cause

March 13, 2008

Detective Smith gave me a "Probable Cause Statement" at the initial hearing held at the County Courthouse in the small town of Jackson, Cape Girardeau County. Outlined was yet more criminal activity, beside the five murders in Missouri. These additional charges being brought to bear were based largely on Krajcir's confessions. As I had not heard much about the Cape crimes up to this point, I was shocked and appalled at the horrific terror he had spread throughout this community.

Item 1 states that "I have probable cause to believe that Timothy W. Krajcir committed one or more criminal offenses."

Item 2 details one of the assaults. "On December 28, 1981," The victim, "M.C., age 24, arrived" home, "at approximately 6 PM". Five young children were there. Soon after, a masked man with a "blue bandana" over his face "forced his way into the residence and ordered everyone onto the floor. The suspect then demanded money. The suspect then ordered M.C. into an adjacent bedroom where she was forced to remove all her clothing. The suspect then digitally penetrated M.C.'s vagina, and subsequently sodomized her. The sodomy included the suspect forcing her to put his penis into her mouth, while he held the handgun to her head.

Item 3 happened on "April 25, 1982, at approximately 9:25 PM". The victim this time was" G.D., age 24, along with her two small children, who were under seven years, and M.L., age 28, were present at the residence of E.S., age 27....Also present in the residence were E.S.'s two small children, who were under the age of seven years. A masked suspect, who was armed with a small handgun, then entered the home and ordered G.D., M.L., and E.S. onto the floor. The suspect then ordered the small children into an adjacent room and closed the door while making verbal threats to them. The suspect then stole a small amount of cash from purses belonging to G.D. and E.S., and a small amount of cash and three rings...from M.L. The suspect then ordered the three women to "undress completely, turn their backs to him, while he sat in a chair and masturbated. The suspect then ordered E.S. to sit on his lap, and shortly thereafter, sodomized her. The sodomy included the suspect forcing her to put his penis into her mouth." Then "the suspect then ordered G.D. over to him, and digitally penetrated her vagina. The suspect then ordered G.D., M.L., and E.S. to lean over a couch with their backs facing him. The suspect then approached, and forced the barrel of the handgun into M.L.'s anus, while he fondled her."

Item 4 happened on May 17, 1982. "At approximately 9:15 PM, a suspect, who was armed with a small handgun, entered the home of E.S., age 79, (now deceased), and his wife, E.U.S., age 62. The suspect ordered the husband and wife onto the floor, and then stole approximately $130.00 cash from them while making threats that he would shoot them if they did not cooperate. The suspect was described as a white male, very dark complexion, 20-30 years of age, 5'8", 130 lbs., slender build, thick black eyebrows, dark eyes, wearing a blue shirt, blue jeans, with a dark colored bandana over the lower part of his face.

In the **Investigative Summary** portion of the report, Detective Smith goes on to say that "In August, 2007, Timothy W. Krajcir, date of birth 11/28/1944, was developed as a suspect in numerous murders, rapes, and other criminal activity, within the city limits of Cape Girardeau, MO.

Subsequent DNA analysis, from physical evidence collected in the 1982 Mildred Wallace murder case, confirmed that Timothy W. Krajcir's DNA could not be excluded from several items of evidence and the probability of the DNA not belonging to Krajcir was only one in 720,000. In addition, notification was received from the Missouri State Highway Patrol Crime Laboratory, that a latent palm print collected from the Wallace murder scene also matched Krajcir."

The report goes on to detail the interviews that took place at Big Muddy Correctional Center in Ina, and the December 3, 2007 meeting where he admitted to "a total of nine murders, which occurred in Missouri, Illinois, and Pennsylvania, giving a full detailed confession to each. "

He goes on to state that "Krajcir further admitted that he came to Cape Girardeau from Illinois for the sole purpose of 'hunting' victims, and often wore a blue bandana during his attacks upon women in Cape Girardeau, MO."

It was also at this time that he admitted the sexual attacks.

An article in the *St. Louis Post-Dispatch*, "They knew they were survivors", dated March 16, 2008, interviewed some of the above-mentioned women. It began in July, 1979, with a woman sleeping on her living room couch after doing some yard work. She awoke to "see Krajcir standing over her...A blue bandana was covered his face." The woman, then 49, was asked "where's your daughter?"

Apparently, Krajcir had "hunted the daughter" and had returned for her. The daughter was not home.

"You'll do," Krajcir said.

According to the article, the victim, now deceased, was asked to "choose how she would be assaulted. She tried to escape. At less than 5 feet tall and 98 pounds, she didn't have a chance. He slammed her to the floor."

Later, she went to one of her grown children's houses. She apparently "asked...for a cup of bleach" to gargle with.

In that same house, on December 28, 1981, two years and five months later, one of this woman's daughters was at the home tending to a small child, "when a rush of cold air burst through the door. She saw a man wearing a blue bandana standing in the doorway with a gun pointed at her family."

A replay of an earlier time, the man asked for her sister, who was not home, again.

So M.C. was told to go into another room. She wanted to fight him, until he turned the gun on her little nephew. She remembers, vividly, her small nephew's big, frightened eyes fastening on hers. She did as her attacker asked.

These two women, mother and daughter, never suspected they were attacked by the same man, or that man was a dangerous serial killer. They had lived. Two more victims would be murdered in the future.

The article in the *Post-Dispatch*, March 16, 2008 also interviewed two of the three women assaulted the evening of April 25, 1982.

These three women, who had been friends for many years, growing up in the area together, had planned a girls-night-out at one of their homes. Unfortunately, this was the home of the woman "hunted" by Krajcir as his next victim. He looked in the window and saw three women together and the chance to live out one of his fantasies.

They had their children in the house. "Suddenly, the children filed into the room. Behind them was a man wearing a blue bandana and pointing a gun at them."

He threatened the children, using them as leverage as he was prone to do. They were locked into a closet.

The women were told to strip, and what had begun as a fun, girls-only night out, quickly descended into a hellish ordeal.

"We had to watch our friends be harmed like that," one of the women told the re-porter.

And, all during the attack they "cried, prayed," and wondered how to "escape".

Of course, they could not very well attempt to leave with the children locked up and at the attacker's mercy. They complied with his demands, as others did, to better ensure the safety and the very lives of their children.

Krajcir apparently was enjoying his little "party", even occasionally sipping from their margarita glasses.

One of the women, married only a short time at the crime's occurrence, stated that "It ruined my marriage. It ruined my life."

Only lately have these women learned the identity of their attacker. True to form, he had picked out a woman and followed her home. But, when he peeped into the window, he saw an opportunity to live out one of his fantasies. He was most likely thrilled to find not one woman, but three.

They and their children lived through a horrific ordeal. Since it is still a mystery to both police and Krajcir himself why some lived and some died at his hands, they can at least count themselves, relatively speaking, lucky to have lived through that hellish evening. These women are true survivors and heroes, having put the safety and welfare of their friends and children before their own.

The last charge dealt with a home invasion of an elderly couple. On May 17, 1982, E.S.was 79 years old. He was at home with his wife. They had been married 40 years. Suddenly a man with a blue bandana, armed with a gun stood before them. He demanded money. E.S. "refused and threatened to slash Krajcir's throat with his pocket knife."

His wife handed over his wallet.

They were told to lie face down on the floor, but were not harmed. They expected a bullet in the back of their heads. Instead, Krajcir left.

Still, Mrs. S. said, "To my husband, it was a matter of principle. Someone overpowered him in our home. I don't think it ever left him. It took something away from him. His pride and self-esteem."

Chapter Fourteen

Plea Hearing and the Victim Impact Statements

April 4, 2008, Federal Building,
Cape Girardeau, Missouri

The April 4, 2008 Court Appearance by Timothy Wayne Krajcir was moved to the downtown Cape Girardeau Federal building on Broadway. From the steep hill the building is perched on, you can clearly see the Mississippi River rolling by at the bottom, just then with its flood swept silt, a wide, fast-flowing stretch of brown colored water. It was a cold and raw day with sullen skies but thankfully no rain, yet.

I paused, briefly, to watch this force of nature flow by, and reflect how indifferent this ancient watercourse was to the varied human dramas unfolding along its banks.

The change from the smaller, older Jackson County Courthouse was better able to accommodate a larger crowd and tighter security. I had a cell phone and a small camera in my purse. Approaching an airport type security set-up, I opened my purse. I was told I could not bring those items in, and must take them out of the building. I would not be admitted until the offending items were gone.

In a steeply hilly town, with a chill wind wrapping my raincoat around my legs, a few blocks can be a bit of a hike. As I had no choice, I walked uphill to my car. Parking was not available very close to the building.

Once back at the courthouse I moved slowly through the security x-ray line. Watch, purse, keys, coat, belt went into the container to be picked up on the other side. We all had to walk through the metal detector just inside the doors. A security guard waited on the other side with a "wand." I passed through without any trouble. The lady behind me had on boots with side zippers. They asked to see her boot-tops to make sure she did not have a weapon tucked away.

The U.S. Marshals were in charge of Krajcir's personal security, and various other county and local police were also along to assist.

The courtroom was upstairs, with a good-sized hall outside for us to congregate in. There was another x-ray machine to go through before we could be admitted to the courtroom.

The crowd grew to about a hundred people, with reporters from television and newspapers mingling in with family members and friends of the deceased and the survivors.

There was a low murmur of quiet conversation in the hall. It reminded me very much of the visitation before a funeral. But today was long after earthly remains had been surrendered. It was a different kind of letting-go these people had come for today. They had come for justice, finally, after all these years.

Some of the people planned on making a statement as to how these crimes had affected their lives and those of their loved ones. Some had brought pictures taken a quarter of a century ago. Some indicated they dreaded seeing Krajcir. Sadness, anxiety, and tension softly palpitated through the crowd.

The hearing was scheduled for 2 p.m., and at 1:30 p.m. the doors to the courtroom opened. We again went through the metal detectors and showed a color-coded card we had been given. There was "assigned seating", it seemed.

As I lined up to go through that last x-ray machine and metal detector check-point, an older lady was just ahead of me. She said she had come with her niece, a friend of the late Brenda Parsh. Her name is Faye Schreiner and she is 75 years young. She had lived in the neighborhood where the killings had taken place in Cape Girardeau. We sat together during the hearing, and talked afterwards.

Standing between the people filing into the courtroom gallery and the gate leading into the inner court area, were at least five security guards. Three tables, in a U-shaped configuration, had been set up there. Of the two tables that faced each other, the left one was for Krajcir and his attorney, and the opposing table was for the detectives, sheriff, and other law enforcement officials, including Lieutenant Echols and Detective Jimmy Smith. In the middle of the room, facing the judge, was a table and a microphone for Krajcir and his attorney to use when addressing the judge and the courtroom.

After we had all been seated, an announcement was made that the doors to the courtroom would be locked. If anyone needed to leave the courtroom for any reason, they would not be re-admitted.

I later learned that the entire Federal building was locked down for the court appearance of Timothy Wayne Krajcir. No one got into or out of the building for over two hours.

The Honorable Judge Benjamin Lewis presided. I was told he was a local, and had known, or known of, a couple of the victims.

Promptly at 2 p.m., Krajcir was brought in, again wearing his prison orange clothing and black rubber glasses. He looked pale, as though he did not see much of the outdoors. He was shackled hand and foot. These were not removed.

Over a dozen burly men in dark jackets spread out. I wondered whether they were wearing protective vests under their jackets, but nevertheless they were still big guys. And armed, of course. The U.S. Marshalls, I guessed. Four took up posts, one directly behind Krajcir, and arrayed to his left.

There had been a couple of times in my personal interactions with Krajcir, when scared out of my wits, I could have used just one of those guys, and they were not to be found for miles and miles. And now here was a courtroom full of them.

I briefly experienced flashbacks: a young mother armed with her gardening tools, frightened but determined; a frantic call to the police for help, my heart hammering while a familiar man in a familiar car sat outside the Witte house; a vivid memory like a photograph of a handgun perched in a notch of a tree overhanging a sandbox.

I glanced around, wondering what was going through the minds of some of the others gathered here. A woman clutched an old photo in her hand, staring down at her lost friend. Family members put their arms around another, drawing close. A woman held a handkerchief to her face as she watched the proceedings.

They were experiencing memories of their own. Most were undoubtedly painful and sad. What if I had checked on her, or gone with her, if I had only done this or that? Some were of regret, having lost someone that they would not grow older with, or someone that would never know children or grandchildren. All of these people, the crowd so large it had spilled over into the jury box, every seat in the courtroom taken, had been impacted so dramatically and hurtfully, by the actions of just one man. And this was only one town, one place Krajcir had "hunted".

Surely, I was seeing this courtroom through a disturbing, distorted looking-glass where every protection was afforded to a violent criminal, and innocent women and helpless children had had to fend for themselves. It seemed surreal.

But, no. This was, indeed, reality.

With the U.S. Marshalls fanning out behind Krajcir and to his left, Krajcir standing at the middle table facing the judge, his attorney close by to his immediate right; the law enforcement people at a table to the attorney's right; and the Judge facing outward toward Krajcir and the audience in the packed courtroom, I had the sense of attending a macabre wedding.

We had our beefy bridesmaids to Krajcir's left, Krajcir himself, his best man, or attorney, and attendants, the law enforcement personnel. The Judge was in the proper position to "pronounce" the sentence. All that was missing was the bride.

Was she there, that day, represented by the often depicted feminine, blindfolded Justice, who we all had come together to see? Or perhaps, Timothy Krajcir's bride could well have been Mercy, who was to be given to this particular groom on this day.

When Morley Swingle agreed to take the death penalty off the table so Krajcir would confess his crimes, all the remaining Cape Girardeau family members had been consulted as to the waiver of the death penalty. The families had to be united on this—and they were, without dissent.

Mercy, "until death do us part."

Each charge against Krajcir was fully explained and the crime detailed. The judge asked him why he was guilty of these crimes. Krajcir would then describe what he had done.

One of the women in the crowd outside the courtroom had stated to me that he had "used Cape Girardeau as his hunting ground", and this did indeed appear to be true. Of course the entire community was terrorized by these crimes.

He described how he would linger on the edges of parking lots, pick out a victim and follow her home. Returning a few days or a week later, he would break into the house and wait for his victim to return. One back door was left open—one back screen was slit. A couple of back windows he broke and climbed in.

A sexual assault survivor from a 1981 attack said during the Impact Statements that he had put a gun to the head of her three-year-old nephew.

She further stated that, "I felt dirty, unclean. I still have a cloud over me."

"Hopefully, today this cloud will break up and go away. I am not afraid any more."

Brenda and Mary Parsh returned home from the local airport to find Krajcir waiting.

In an email from Detective Jimmy Smith dated 5/14/08 in response to my having asked for clarification of a couple of items, he stated that "Krajcir was in (Mary Parsh's) neighborhood in early August 1977. (He) saw her arrive home and…then looked through her windows and assured himself that she lived alone. He went back to the home approximately two weeks later, (08/12/77), saw the car was gone, and broke into the home through a back bedroom window. He waited in the master bedroom for Mrs. Parsh to arrive home. He did not know that Brenda would be with her mother."

I always wondered what Krajcir was doing while lurking inside of people's houses, waiting for his victims to come home. Did he not look in the closet, at least this time, and see men's clothing hanging there? Did he paw through the women's underwear? Did he masturbate? We know he stole from his victims whenever he could. Was he on a search for valuables he could take with him when he was finished with this next victim?

Detective Smith goes on to say that he was armed with a .38 pistol and he must have "accosted them as they entered the front door. Suit cases were left just inside the door, and house keys were found in the door knob."

Even having spent so little time around the Cape Girardeau families and neighbors, I knew without a doubt that Mary was very proud of her beautiful daughter, Brenda; Detective Smith said she was "definitely very proud of Brenda. Mary was likely subdued prior to Krajcir's assault on Brenda."

Because Krajcir used others as leverage to better gain compliance with his wishes, perhaps he threatened to kill Mary if the daughter did not cooperate. Krajcir later said Brenda was fairly calm, but Mary was not, initially.

"Krajcir remembered the telephone rang while he was forcing Brenda to perform oral sex. He then escorted her into the other room and permitted her to answer. It was her father inquiring why she did not call him upon her arrival. Krajcir was listening while holding his pistol to Brenda's head. Krajcir recalled part of the conversation and remembered that Brenda told him that she was tired and would see him the following day. (She) then made an excuse as to why her mother could not come to the phone. Krajcir recalled Brenda telling her father, 'I love you daddy, and I will see you tomorrow'."

Mr. Parsh was in the hospital, just having undergone open-heart surgery. Brenda had come home to see him.

He would not see his bright, lively daughter again, or his wife, either. How he recovered from his surgery and found the will to go on living is beyond me. No surgery, unfortunately, could repair his now permanently broken heart from such grievous loss.

Krajcir then took Brenda back to the bedroom where her Mother was presumably restrained. He finished his sexual assault, raping her on the bed beside her Mother, who had also been forced to disrobe. They were at this point both bound with their hands behind their backs; face down, on the bed. Krajcir shot Brenda first, killing her with a shot to the back of the head. He shot Mrs. Parsh in the back of the head, or so he thought. He missed, wounding her.

Leaving the bedroom, Krajcir went looking for things to

steal. The house having gone quiet, Mary probably assumed, incorrectly, that the intruder was gone and began giving in to her shock and horror of this unbelievable ordeal in her very own home. She began to cry.

Krajcir, alarmed at the sounds coming from the bedroom, rushed back. Mary, hearing his approach, realized too late her mistake. Helplessly bound, naked on the bed beside her murdered daughter, she must have felt, yet again, a cold wash of terror. Krajcir, taking more careful aim this time, shot her in the back of the head, killing her in cold blood.

Brenda was a pretty girl, and Faye's niece had shared some photographs of her and Brenda. One was of the two of them together. Brenda had a sparkling tiara on her head. Brenda, a close friend, was also a bridesmaid in her wedding.

During the Victim Impact Statement she made, she said that Brenda came from a "very meager background."She indicated Mary had worked very hard to provide the wherewithal for Brenda to be able pursue the pageant circuit. Everyone in the courtroom was painfully aware that a treasured daughter of a proud mother was brutalized and killed right before her eyes by the man sitting impassively before us in an orange jumpsuit.

If only, we all wished, Mary could have passed out or gone into shock and been struck dumb, just until Krajcir had left the house, she could have described the attacker. Probably she would never have rested until he was brought to justice. Krajcir just couldn't take the chance on leaving a living witness.

Brenda's friend ended her statement to the court by saying positively, that "Brenda definitely would have made a difference in society if she had been allowed to live."

As for Shelia Cole, the college student from the St. Louis area attending college in Cape Girardeau, Krajcir "hunted" her at a Wal-Mart parking lot off Kingshighway in Cape.

She was in her car in the parking lot. A large truck or van was blocking the view of her car from the front of the store. Krajcir approached and pointed the gun at her and told her to get into his car. She did as he ordered.

He forced her into the back of his car telling her she would not be hurt if she cooperated. He took her across state lines to his trailer in Carbondale, Illinois, where he sexually assaulted her.

Driving back toward Missouri, he pulled into a roadside rest stop in a deserted and remote area, taking Sheila into the stall with him at gunpoint, making her turn around. When he was finished, he shot her. When she fell to the floor, he shot her again, this time killing her. He left her body there like trash.

Both of Shelia Cole's parents are now deceased. Before her mother died, her father had once again called the police to report that his wife was dying and begged for any information. They did not have anything new or anything at all, really, to give to this couple who had never ceased to grieve for their cherished, murdered daughter. The father then too passed away, wondering every day what had happened to his daughter, badly needing some sort of resolution for his broken heart and receiving none.

During his confessions to the police, Krajcir stated he "was not sure" if he could kill Brenda and Mary Parsh and Shelia Cole. Of course, he did.

Don Call is the surviving son of Marjorie Call, whom Krajcir strangled in January, 1982. His brother died a couple of years ago and so did not live to see justice for his mother. Mr. Call said they both had lived since 1982 with a sense of guilt that they were not there to protect her. He said their jobs had taken them away from Cape Girardeau and they were not able to see about her during the week, only on weekends.

He stated that for them both, "The overwhelming question" was "Why was our Mother murdered?" Here Mr. Call broke down in tears. He continued, "Now we know she was murdered simply for being in the wrong place at the wrong time."

Krajcir hunted Mrs. Call at the Kroger parking lot. He followed her into the store and bought his favorite brand of rawhide boot laces to tie her with right then and there. He followed her home.

He peeped into her window. No sign of a man in residence. So far, so good. He would return about a week later, breaking a bathroom window. She was not home, but returned in about 30 minutes or so. She had gone into the bathroom upon her return and immediately felt a draft and then saw the broken window. She probably realized she was not alone in the house and ran for the front door, but Krajcir caught up with her.

To stop her screaming, Krajcir stuffed a dry wash cloth down her throat. Even though he was armed with a gun, he strangled her after assaulting her in the bedroom. And, for some unknown reason, after she was dead, he cut off one of her nipples. Possibly he felt that by trying to escape, she had defied him. Krajcir made his victims pay for any perceived act of defiance. "I was going to take it as a souvenir," he told the court.

But then not knowing what he was going to do with his grisly prize, he flushed it down the toilet. He also went through some church envelopes and took the money. He left through the back door of the house, strolled through the carport, and was once again back out into the welcoming night he was so comfortable with.

Mildred Wallace, age 65 in June of 1982 was Krajcir's last victim.

He again was on the Kroger lot, hunting.

He followed her home, peeping into her windows. He was familiar with the area by now, as all of his Cape Girardeau victims came from a relatively small area in the same part of town. He noticed she was going to leave again, so he waited until she left. He broke a window with a brick he found laying on the ground. As he climbed into the house, he cut his hand on the broken glass, leaving his DNA at the crime scene. Over twenty years later, this was the break the Cape Girardeau police would need to link Krajcir to the Deborah Sheppard murder in Carbondale, Illinois.

Krajcir tried to correct his previous mistakes. He cut the phone cord, so the phone would not interrupt him as it did with Brenda Parsh. He also stuffed a towel into the broken window so she would not notice stray breezes or noises as had Marjorie Call, who nearly got away from him as she bolted towards her front door. He found a band-aid for his cut. He waited.

A few minutes later, when Mildred Wallace returned home she was pounced on in her bedroom. Krajcir said, "She asked me if I was the guy who killed the woman across town." He denied it.

After he assaulted her, he told her to stay on her bed where she was blindfolded. He ransacked her things looking for valuables or money, and when he was done he shot her in the head. He walked calmly out into the night, murder having become commonplace to him by now.

The random violence Krajcir could and did visit upon those who had crossed his path is stunning, even after all these years.

Krajcir sat at the defendant's table, facing the detectives and jury box with his attorney during the victims' statements. I watched him fairly closely. I saw no reaction to the words or tears of these family members, victims, or friends. Although some in the audience swore they saw that he did shed a tear or two, I personally did not. For the most part, Krajcir was sitting as impassively as if he were watching television.

But when Marjorie Call's nephew, Chuck Bertling, stepped up to the microphone, he referenced the death penalty that was not being given to Krajcir. He said, with much feeling that even so, he "hopes you rot in the fiery fires of hell!"

As Chuck Bertling turned away from the mike and strode purposely to his seat, Krajcir involuntarily jerked, twice.

Krajcir was brought back to the microphone, facing the judge. With his back to the crowded gallery, he stated, "I heard what they said."

His voice was raspy and it broke at this point. He said he had had "intense therapy" and had done some "terrible acts".

He continued, "I would like to apologize to (the) victims and families in Cape Girardeau for the terror I caused."

He acknowledged that had the "situation been reversed, I don't know if I could've been so generous," referring to the unanimous rejection by the five murdered victims' families to waive the death penalty.

"I'm terribly sorry for what I've done. I can feel your pain."

He also pledged to be a counselor to other sexual offenders so these types of things would not happen again.

Skeptical, I wondered how this would come about. As a now-designated serial killer he will be held in a maximum security prison with little or no contact with other inmates, locked away with others of his ilk who are simply irredeemable and cannot be let loose against society ever again. At least, for one newspaper reporter, his statement that he was "sorry" made for good newspaper copy.

The Judge, upon passing sentence on each individual count gave Krajcir 13 life sentences. These will be served consecutively, meaning each one must be served before the next sentence can begin. Reflecting upon the heinous nature and deliberation given to his crimes, the 13 life sentences seem more than justified.

In the words of the Judge, Krajcir would "never draw another breath as a free man."

The hearing ended at 3:30 p.m.

The indomitable Faye Schreiner, my seatmate during the long hearing, had in early 1977 just completed a move back to Cape Girardeau, Missouri after unexpectedly finding herself a young widow of a police officer in Chicago, Illinois. At 34, and with a young son to raise, she had packed up and moved back to more familiar surroundings. With long red hair and at about 120 pounds, she was a looker.

She knew the Parsh family and Margie Call. She lived in the same vicinity as they did. After being back for just three months, the first murders occurred, those of the Parsh women one and a half blocks away.

The police came around, much as they did in Marion after the death of Virginia Witte.

Her next-door neighbor, an elderly woman was so scared she had a breakdown.

Faye would soon move again, and was eager to do so after a frightening incident that occurred the weekend the Parsh murders took place. Faye received a telephone call from a strange man.

"He had a real flirty, young voice," she said. He told her he was "starting a stud service up and he would give her real cheap rates." She asked his name and he replied, "John Lukeshaw".

Just as a neighbor woman on Lakeview had received an anonymous telephone call from a man identifying himself with both a first and last name the weekend after Virginia's murder, and as I had received a telephone call from a man, also identifying himself with a first and last name clustered right after the murders, so did Faye.

Faye was so new to the neighborhood that her telephone number was not in the current telephone directory. And, while not an unlisted number, someone would have had to make a point of finding it, perhaps from directory assistance inquiring about a new number listing. Her curiosity was piqued; she asked him how he knew her.

He said, "Honey, I know everything about you."

He described her and even told her what kind of car she drove. Had he seen Faye out and about, perhaps followed her home from a grocery store while she and her young son went about their errands, unaware they were being watched?

None of us believed the made-up names, either first or last. The timing and the names were coincidental, however.

One more coincidence came up from my talk with Faye Schreiner. Margie Call, who lived just two blocks from Faye, had called police to report cigarette butts found around her air conditioner unit, under a window in the back yard. She lived alone and did not smoke. The area was not well lit, so she was concerned.

I did have a flash-back to tweezers picking up an unexplained cigarette butt from underneath my own kitchen window beside the air conditioning unit, and placing it in an evidence bag.

The police told Call there was nothing they could do about it; it could have been a utility worker.

We know Krajcir lurked in neighborhoods at night, particularly backyards where he could not be seen by passer-by, and he liked dimly lit areas. The police have told me he "knew things about his victims", and Krajcir has volunteered the information that he followed women home from grocery stores, and various parking lots, returning a few days or a week later to commit his crime. He has also admitted to being a "Peeping Tom" and masturbating while doing so.

Perhaps he knows more than he has actually admitted to so far, although what he has admitted to is plenty. It is no wonder Faye says women did not walk the streets. Cape Girardeau, Missouri has the dubious distinction of having had the most murders by Timothy Krajcir, two (the Parsh women) in August of 1977; Shelia Cole in November 1977; January of 1982, Marjorie Call; and again in 1982 his final victim from Cape, Mildred Wallace.

Outside the courtroom, a sexual assault survivor who had made an emotional statement during the impact statement portion of the hearing said she "did not believe" Krajcir was "sorry" as she angrily wiped away tears.

Faye, not convinced that Krajcir's "I'm sorry for what I've done" was all that heartfelt, either, sidled up to one of the Federal Marshalls and asked him if he thought Krajcir really was all that sorry.

The Marshall's reply was, "Ma'am, he's a serial killer. If he gets out, he will do it again."

Chapter Fifteen

The Last Victim

Is there yet one more, largely forgotten victim of serial killer Timothy Krajcir?

A very recent development has been the confessions of Krajcir to three additional crimes in Mt. Vernon, Illinois, about 45 miles north of Marion along Interstate 57. Two were rapes, and it is unclear if the victims ever did come forward. Existing complaints do not seem to match up to the confessions.

One attack is currently in dispute, the person convicted of this attempted murder having since died in prison. The Mt. Vernon police are maintaining, at the time of this writing, that Krajcir has given a false confession.

Grover W. Thompson, the man convicted of the multiple stabbing and attempted murder of one Ida White, was passing through town via Greyhound bus when apprehended. He was on a layover and had taken shelter inside the unlocked outer lobby of the Post Office. Unfortunately, this was just across the street from Ms. White's apartment. He was convicted of the multiple stabbing and attempted murder of Ida White in 1981. Ms. White was 72 at the time of the attack on Labor Day, 1981. These events took place at night, around 9:20 p.m.

According to Lieutenant Echols, and Detective Tina Morrow, Krajcir gave details that only a person at the scene of the crime could have knowledge of. One detailed item was where the assailant was hiding in the apartment; the other detailed a phone conversation Ida White had just had before getting ready for bed. The telephone conversation has definitely checked out.

It also fits the "M.O.", or mode of operation, of Krajcir. He was most active at night.

The Mt. Vernon police have put forth the defense that they all but caught the suspect at the scene of the crime, lingering in the lobby of the neighboring Post Office building with a bloody knife. He was tried and convicted, serving 14 years of his sentence before he died.

A neighbor had heard Ida's cries for help and may have helped saved her life. He said that he chased the man from her apartment and gave a description. Ms. White only said her attacker was black.

I tracked down the then-court appointed public defender for Grover Thompson, Steven Swofford, who was working in Murphysboro, Illinois, for his comment. Per Mr. Swofford, police found Grover Thompson just across the street from Ida White's apartment. He was tired from traveling all day on a Greyhound bus, and asked the bus agent if he could take another bus out the next morning. Told he could, he set out to find a place to rest for a few hours. He found the unlocked Post Office lobby in the next block, and curled up under a table. He was found and arrested within 30 minutes of the police arriving on the scene. He was found to have in his possession a pocketknife with a small drop of blood on it. The drop of blood was so tiny it defied analysis. Mr. Thompson said it was his blood, but this could not be proven at the time.

Mr. Swofford has always been passionate in his belief in Grover Thompson's innocence, and remains so today. He indicated to me that some evidence had been suppressed during the trial.

Much as I always thought something would turn up in the murder of Virginia Witte, Stephen Swofford had felt the same way, too, about his client, Grover Thompson. Neither one of us thought it would ever come so late that so many of those who cared, who mattered, would be gone to their graves.

He said he "always thought something would happen. (I) had a feeling that this guy was innocent."

Swofford was invited to view the taped confession by Krajcir of his attempted murder of Ida White. Since then, he is absolutely certain that his former client was innocent of the crime he was convicted of.

And, the interview conducted by a detective from the Mt. Vernon police ended abruptly. The detective professed not to believe Krajcir's confession to the stabbing and started to leave. Krajcir lost his temper, yelling, "Get that guy back in here," then offering to take a lie detector test to prove he *did* do it.

I told Swofford about the hearing in Cape I had attended, and how sincere Krajcir had sounded. I wondered out loud why he would bother to confess to other crimes beyond the murders for which they had DNA evidence (Deborah Sheppard and Mildred Wallace and Shelia Cole). I was somewhat baffled that he was willing to confess to these crimes so he would *not* face the death penalty. It seemed to me he was simply going to spend the rest of his life in jail, whether he was on death row or not. As a prisoner in his 60s, his life might very well end before his appeals ran out. I reflected that Krajcir apparently places a far higher value on his own life than he did on those of his victims.

Stephen Swofford immediately countered with, "If you had committed 60 rapes, and nine murders, would *you* be in a hurry to meet your maker?"

He has a very good point.

Conclusion

So, a tale that, for me, began thirty years ago in May, 1978, as a young mother happily planting marigolds in her front yard on a beautiful spring day, ends with the final sentencing on April 4, 2008, of what we know now is a serial killer and a dangerous sexual predator.

How could one life, that of Timothy Krajcir, possibly have caused so much fear, misery and even death for so many others?

The impact on the family members who were left behind, some of whom went to their graves not knowing who, or why, their daughters, wives, mothers, girlfriends, sisters or friends were brutalized and murdered, is palpable in their anguish.

The years have not taken that away, perhaps they have dimmed it, but it is always there, the question, "Why?"

Why indeed. The answer to the question as to who lived and who died was often a whim of Krajcir's.

Was he particularly careful?

No. He went back to the same area in Cape Girardeau numerous times. He lurked around houses, peeping into windows. He broke windows and entered homes waiting for his victim to come home. He cruised through neighborhoods and loitered on parking lots. People noticed. When he went into Virginia Witte's house, he left the middle bedroom window open. If one of the neighbors who lived in between our houses had been home, they could have heard something going on inside that house.

He did plan his crimes to a certain extent, at least as much as humanly possible. He had his buck knife, and his bandana and leather shoelaces, and sometimes a clipboard or box, pretending to be a delivery person. He scouted out his victims, following them home and returning a few days or maybe even a week or two later to attack at a time of his choosing.

He had, as the saying goes, "The luck of the Devil". He just missed meeting Virginia's husband returning home. He did not get a call from the Marion police department about his car when his name appeared on the dealer list requested by and submitted to the police. He was not called in for questioning after he was observed by the personnel sent to his trailer in Carbondale by the Marion police, although Krajcir's physical description and that of his car matched both Connie Clark's and my statements to the police. To the best of my knowledge their report was never forwarded, or noticed, or referenced, by the Detectives working on the case. Nor, again to the best of my knowledge, was the report by the State Police Special Agent as to vehicle purchase and Krajcir's workplace and work hours followed up on, nor the parole officer's tip. My frantic phone call requesting help immediately as to the man sitting outside and just north of the Witte house a short time after the murder, is not even notated in the case file. The Detective I tried to reach apparently never got the message; a patrol car was not dispatched, even though it would have been too late to detain Krajcir then. All these things just got lost in the huge pile of evidence and leads, perhaps, and a serial killer remained at large.

Also, the focus by all the police forces grappling with all these unsolved assaults, murders, and robberies was local, first and foremost. At the Cape Girardeau hearing, I heard several people say that they had wondered at the time who knew this victim or that one, and who would have killed her? The first assumption was that it had to have been someone who was known to the victim and therefore local, not a sexual predator "commuting" from Carbondale, Illinois.

The fact that Krajcir himself did not always know what triggered his "hunting" to hone in on a particular woman, and who would drive within a certain radius to look for victims and commit crimes, was not particularly helpful to solving these crimes.

This was before DNA was available, too.

As we all know, hindsight is a wonderful thing. For whom, I have never been quite sure.

Those of us who unwittingly crossed paths with this cruel, evil person and lived to tell about it are indeed fortunate. Many women probably slipped by him, and for those that lived through a brutal assault or robbery, not to minimize their trauma over the passing years, even they were luckier than some.

Yes, they were terrorized and hurt, left fearful or even angry, but they are *survivors* nevertheless. It has indeed been hard for nearly everyone to take up their lives again after encountering Timothy Krajcir. Hopefully they can reject the label of *victim* that everyone uses to describe them as, and see themselves as strong survivors, instead. Surely, if they can get through the terrible ordeal that an encounter with Timothy Krajcir most certainly was, they can be confident that they can get through pretty much of anything.

And, it may be a telling glimpse into the inner workings of an intelligent and manipulative man that we see Krajcir enter his guilty pleas in a relatively closed and protected environment and preferring to avoid a trial-by-jury.

Always secretive, lurking in the shadows, needing control, "hunting" unaware, innocent victims, it was in his nature to try to have some say as to how the final courtroom dramas would unfold.

He could have pled "not guilty", and the prosecutors would then have geared up for trials—for lengthy, gritty, and unpleasant scrutiny of Krajcir and his deeds.

From the first interviews with Lieutenant Paul Echols and Detective Jimmy Smith and others, Krajcir first denied his involvement in any of the crimes they sought answers for. When Detective Smith first indicated the death penalty could be taken off the table, Krajcir was able, at last, to give details of the crimes. And, it appears he most certainly did not want anyone else to take credit for his handiwork, as reflected by Krajcir's losing his temper when the detective from Mt. Vernon claimed he did not believe his confession to the stabbing of Ida White.

He had had years to think that eventually someone would come around asking about some of his criminal activities, and to plan for it. He must have known this deal was the best he would get.

The trials that could have taken place have certainly saved the taxpayers a lot of money. But it has also kept information as to the crimes committed out of the public eye. This self-absorbed, compulsive and driven man's thoughts and deeds would have been scrutinized. Krajcir would have been totally exposed, step-by-step, for all to see.

Not only would the news media have reported on his actions, but real people, the people in the courtroom and the jury would have reflected back onto Krajcir their shock at, and repugnance of, his crimes. Imagine the reaction of a jury to a prosecutor's statement that he held a gun to a toddler's head.

Imagine how the crimes against the Parsh women would seem presented by a rigorous prosecution.

Would the words of the prosecutor, hammering home the heinous crimes he committed have held up a mirror to Krajcir, so he would have to see himself as others see him? Would he not be exposed for all to see, this dark, twisted individual, as he truly is? Could he have looked into that reflective mirror, and acknowledged, fully, what he has done and know that he feels no remorse, really, and is therefore lacking in basic humanity? Or is he incapable of even seeing his own reflection at all?

We will never know what any trial would have brought about. As Krajcir himself stated at the Cape Girardeau hearing when he confessed to multiple murders, he did not know, if the situation had been reversed, that he could have "been so generous" as to disallow the death penalty.

In an email I received from Detective Christina Morrow of the Marion police, she expressed satisfaction that Krajcir was sentenced. She feels that every day he is incarcerated he will be able to reflect on the victims and that to her is justice.

Everyone concerned has agreed that a form of justice has been served. We know he will never be free again for the remainder of his life. He will die in prison.

The American justice system that is often derided by other countries as being too barbaric for our stand on the death penalty should take note of the example set by the surviving family members in Cape Girardeau who allowed Timothy Krajcir to live.

This was not only justice served, but evil trounced by good; caring and compassion for others over cold, remorseless cruelty. It has contrasted the innocent with the evil; the remorseless killer with good, decent people who spared Krajcir's life to bring comfort and closure to others; the dedication of the police and the legal system to their communities, and the imposition of the law over one who views right and wrong and human life as having no value.

As for me, as Detective Morrow once suggested, as I began to write this, it has served as a sort of catharsis. It has also, I hope, spotlighted this individual's horrific crimes. People will know what he is truly capable of, and who he really is.

This is justice to me.

Appendix

A Timeline for Timothy Krajcir

S O WE HAVE A ROADMAP, SO TO SPEAK OF SOME OF THE CRIMES COMMITTED by this dangerous person, I would like to interject a timeline of his criminal activities.

I think it will also help to explain why there are so many unanswered questions concerning the activities of Krajcir.

Lieutenant Echols has put together his own timeline, which is far more complex, and which he says has taken a lot of time and is updated often.

TIMELINE FOR TIMOTHY W. KRAJCIR
(Partly obtained from the Carbondale Police Department Investigative Report RE: Murder of Deborah Sheppard, dated August 21, 2007.)

Timothy Krajcir was born in Mahoney City, PA, 11-28-1944
- Age 13, "in trouble"
- January 29, 1962: Enlists in Navy at age 18
- 1963: Marries in February
- May 10, 1963: rapes and stabs a woman with a 10-inch pair of scissors. She survives, seriously injured.
- 1963: Second rape is also noted in this time frame, while married and living in the North Chicago area.
- 1963: Dishonorable discharged from the Navy. Sent to prison for sexually assaulting a North Chicago woman

and stabbing a Waukegan woman in an attempted sexual attack.

- 1963: Daughter born to his brief, failed marriage.
- 1972: Prior to his parole Krajcir has EMT training. Subsequently works at hospitals in Cairo, Illinois, also Union County in Anna, Illinois, and Doctor's Hospital in Carbondale, Illinois
- June 2, 1974: Obtains A.A. degree from Shawnee Community College.
- 1974: Krajcir changes his name legally to McBride. His biological father's last name was McBride. Apparently his father was a Marine in World War II, but he never knew his biological father. Krajcir was the last name of his stepfather, who helped Fern Krajcir, mother, raise him.
- In prison, to be released in 1976
- 1977: two burglaries in Carbondale (*Southern Illinoisan*, Saturday, January 19, 2008.)
- April 12, 1977: Mary and Brenda Parsh shot in back of head in Cape Girardeau, MO (Tuesday, Dec. 11, 2007 *St. Louis Post-Dispatch*, St. Charles Edition)
- Nov. 16,1977: Southeast Missouri State University student Shelia Cole abducted from a Wal-Mart parking lot, Cape Girardeau, MO, and shot twice in back of head (Tuesday Dec. 11, 2007 *St Louis Post-Dispatch*, St. Charles Edition)
- May 12, 1978: Virginia Witte is murdered in Marion, Illinois
- 1979: murder in his home State of Pennsylvania
- 1979: kidnapping and assault and murder of Joyce Tharp in Paducah, KY. Ms. Tharp was murdered in Krajcir's trailer home West of Carbondale, Illinois. (Interview with Lt. Paul Echols, Jan. 30, 2008) Cause of death, blow to head, strangulation, or both. (*St. Louis Post-Dispatch*, December 15, 2007.)
- 1979: Woman raped in Carbondale, Illinois (statement by Lt. Paul Echols to *Southern Illinoisan*, Saturday, January 19, 2008)
- Krajcir in prison

158

- September 7, 1981: Krajcir admitted to the stabbing attack on Ida White. Grover Thompson convicted for this crime in 1982. (*St. Louis Post-Dispatch*, St. Charles edition, February 17, 2008, "A Case of Justice Denied?")
- January, 1982: woman attacked and sexually assaulted in fornt of her 10 year-old daughter, bound, survived (*St. Louis Post Dispatch*, Dec. 11, 2007, St. Charles edition)
- January 27, 1982: Margie Call found in her home in Cape Girardeau, MO, strangled to death. (*Ibid.*)
- April 8, 1982: Deborah Sheppard found in her Carbondale, IL apartment, strangled and blows to the head. (*Ibid.*)
- June 21, 1982: Mildred Wallace shot once in the head, Cape Girardeau, MO
- 1982: Krajcir admits three assaults around or in 1982 in the Mt. Vernon, IL area. Twice armed with a gun, third time used a knife to stab his victim. (January 19, 2008, *Southern Illinoisan*)
- Krajcir returned to prison for parole violations
- 1988: Enters Big Muddy Correctional Center as a habitual sex offender, where he was when Lieutenant Paul Echols interviewed him concerning Deborah Sheppard (murdered in 1982) case in 2007
- December 12, 2007: Krajcir moved to Tamms Correctional Center after confessions and upgraded to serial killer from sexual offender. Tamms is a maximum security prison. (*St. Louis Post-Dispatch*, December 15, 2007, "Serial killer getting a cell of his own")

About the Author

BONNEY HOGUE PATTERSON and her husband live in St. Charles County, Missouri, and have two children and five grandchildren.

She and her husband both graduated from Mt. Vernon Township High School, in Mt. Vernon, Illinois, and attended and graduated from Eastern Illinois University in Charleston, Illinois. During nearly four decades of marriage, have lived in small towns as well as a few bigger ones—Chicago, St. Louis, and Hong Kong.

They take great delight in their family and extended family and friends.